This picture is of ***Our Lady of America.*** For more information regarding these approved messages, you may email:
www.OurLadyofAmerica.org
You can also write to:
B.V.M. Our Lady of America
c/o Langsenkamp Family Apostolate
6720 Parkdale Place
Indianapolis, IN 46254

THE PREPARATION for the REIGN of the SACRED HEART of JESUS THROUGH the IMMACULATE HEART of MARY

Dedication

This manual is dedicated to the Immaculate Heart of Mary and also to my mother who has shown me, through her example and love, what the Immaculate Heart of Mary must be like!

Also dedicated to Pope Benedict XVI, in honor of his love for the Blessed Virgin Mary, our life, our sweetness and our hope!

The Preparation for the Reign of the Sacred Heart of Jesus Through the Immaculate Heart of Mary

A Preparation for Total Consecration to Mary According to
the Themes Found in Saint Louis Marie De Montfort's Preparation
for the Thirty-Three Day Consecration

By
Kariann LaMarca

BIBLIOGRAPHY

True Devotion To The Blessed Virgin
By St. Louis Marie Grignion De Montfort
Montfort Publications
Bay Shore, NY 11706

The Holy Bible
Revised Standard Version Catholic Edition
Copyright © 1965 and 1966 by the Division of Christian Education of the National Council of the Churches of Christ in the United States of America. Published by Thomas Nelson Publishers for Ignatius Press. All rights reserved.

Catechism of the Catholic Church
Excerpts from the English translation of the Catechism of the Catholic Church for the United States of America Copyright © 1994, United States Catholic Conference – Libreria Editrice Vaticana. All rights reserved.

English translation of the Catechism of the Catholic Church for the United States of America copyright © 1994, United States Catholic Conference, Inc. – Libreria Editrice Vaticana

Copyright © 2007 Kariann LaMarca

TABLE OF CONTENTS

PREFACE   *iv*
INTRODUCTION   *vii*
SPECIAL FEAST FOR CONSECRATION   *xii*

First Period
The Twelve Preliminary Days
Renouncement of the Spirit of the World

First Day	*5*
Second Day	*10*
Third Day	*14*
Fourth Day	*17*
Fifth Day	*21*
Sixth Day	*25*
Seventh Day	*28*
Eighth Day	*32*
Ninth Day	*35*
Tenth Day	*38*
Eleventh Day	*42*
Twelfth Day	*47*

Second Period
First Week
Knowledge of Self

Thirteenth Day	*55*
Fourteenth Day	*59*
Fifteenth Day	*64*
Sixteenth Day	*68*
Seventeenth Day	*72*
Eighteenth Day	*76*
Nineteenth Day	*80*

Third Period
Third Week
Knowledge of the Blessed Virgin

Twentieth Day	*89*
Twenty-First Day	*94*
Twenty-Second Day	*102*
Twenty-Third Day	*107*
Twenty-Fourth Day	*115*
Twenty-Fifth Day	*122*
Twenty-Sixth Day	*129*

Fourth Period
Fourth Week
Knowledge of Jesus Christ

Twenty-Seventh Day	*138*
Twenty-Eighth Day	*141*
Twenty-Ninth Day	*148*
Thirtieth Day	*152*
Thirty-First Day	*157*
Thirty-Second Day	*161*
Thirty-Third Day	*166*

Prayers and Practices

Biblical Foundations of True Devotion	*176*
Prayers	*188*
Litanies	*196*
Renewal of Baptismal Vows	*208*
Act of Consecration	*209*
Special Prayers and Practices	*213*
Mysteries of the Holy Rosary	*215*
Suggestions For Further Reading	*230*

PREFACE

"It was never written that anyone became a saint without having a special devotion to the Blessed Mother." St. Bonaventure

The late Pope John Paul II, shortly before he died in his homily on the Feast of the Baptism of the Lord in January 2005, invited us to a renewed commitment to the new evangelization through a renewed understanding of the sacrament of Baptism. He explained that, "A Christian's mission begins with baptism. Rediscovering baptism through appropriate adult catechesis is an important part of the new evangelization."

As part of this "new evangelization," I believe that St. Louis De Montfort's consecration to Jesus through Mary answers this call of the "new evangelization." This consecration to Jesus through Mary according to St. De Montfort is a perfect renewal of our baptismal vows, through the Blessed Mother. Our baptismal vows are the most important commitment we make to God, therefore it is good for us to renew our baptismal vows even on a yearly basis, according to this method. In addition, there should be a commitment to pray an act of consecration to Jesus through Mary on a daily basis. This act of consecration is a life long journey to the Father with the Blessed Mother at our side and in our hearts. It has been noted that in the history of the Church at times when it was in moral decline, the Shepard's of the Catholic Church had its members renew their baptismal vows. Today, as we look around us, both in the world and in the Church, we see this same moral chaos. Our society has become pagan and it has built up idols for itself such as: pleasure, money, pride, unbridled egoism, impurity, hatred and violence. The world is simply experiencing such a rebellion against God that has not been matched since the beginning of the world. It is heading down the path of its own self-destruction, ruin and death. The world around us is building up for itself a new civilization without God by extolling the idols of materialism, secularism, radical individualism, hedonism, theoretical and practical atheism. It rules with its dictatorship of moral relativism. All this is propagated by the means of mass communication, which extols sin as a good. The Catholic Church has been influenced by the world and has compromised with it. Within the Church herself, she is experiencing among her members a lack of faith, which has caused the spread of apostasy, schism and division. Today, we are witnessing a haughty and open opposition to the teachings of the Magesterium by its own members, even among the hierarchy.

As we look at the reality of our present situation at this time in our history, one could easily become dishearten, discouraged and without hope. To this I respond with the words of Pope John Paul II when he said in response to this present crisis, "DO NOT BE AFRAID." Jesus is with us and the gates of hell shall not prevail against the Church (Matt. 16:18). In addition, we have the great promise spoken by of Our Lady of Fatima, "that in the end my Immaculate Heart will triumph." The Blessed Mother has come to warn us of the grave situation that the world and the Catholic Church find itself in and she has come with the remedy for our ills. In all of her apparitions throughout the last two centuries, her remedy has been the same: prayer, penance, a return to the frequent reception of the sacraments, especially those of Confession and the Holy Eucharist and finally, she has asked for consecration to her Immaculate Heart. This consecration that she asks of us is a perfect renewal of our baptismal vows. She is asking us to re-commit our lives to Jesus through her. Why to Jesus through her Immaculate Heart? We go to Jesus through Mary because this is the way Jesus wishes to establish His reign in the world and most especially in our hearts. "For the Kingdom of God is within you." (Luke 17:21) As St. De Montfort tells us in *True Devotion to the Blessed Virgin Mary*, number 1, "It was through the Blessed Virgin Mary that Jesus Christ came into the world, and it is also through her that he must reign in the world." The Blessed and Adorable Trinity has given the Blessed Virgin Mary to be our mother and has given her the task of forming us into the likeness of Jesus her Son. The more people respond to this invitation of consecration to Jesus through Mary (which is a life long endeavor) the sooner will Christ establish His reign among us. So than let us do what Pope John Paul II commanded us at the dawn of the new millennium, "Let us throw open the doors to Christ who is coming."

"Behold, I make all things new." Revelation 21:5
"Surely I am coming soon." Amen. Come, Lord Jesus!"
Revelation 22:20

INTRODUCTION

Purpose of this Manual

The purpose of this manual is to bring people into a deeper spiritual understanding of how to prepare and live out St. De Montfort's total consecration to Jesus through Mary. St. De Montfort suggests that we take four weeks in order to prepare ourselves for this consecration to Jesus through Mary, which as he states is a "renewal of our baptismal vows." For each week St. De Montfort assigns a "theme" to focus on spiritually. After many years of renewing the consecration, I found that these "themes" are biblically based and found scattered throughout the New Testament.

So for example, you will find more use of Sacred Scripture that corresponds to the different "themes" of this preparation. You will find that the *Catechism of the Catholic Church* has been implemented in order to help further explain what the Church teaches explicitly about the scripture passages for each day. Therefore, one will need to have the *Catechism of the Catholic Church* in order to follow along. Even though one should have read *True Devotion* before making your act of consecration, I have incorporated more of the writings of *True Devotion* for each day of the week for those who may not have able to read it. This has been done because, of the invaluable insights of the writings of St. De Montfort on the doctrine behind Marian spirituality and consecration to Jesus through Mary. At the end of the manual there is a section called, "Special Prayers and Practices." In this section I have added more prayers and spiritual practices that have been allowed to be implemented by the Catholic Church that will enhance your devotion to the Blessed Mother. These practices were something that came about after the death of St. De Montfort, which I am sure that if he were still alive today, would have encouraged such practices. Finally, I have dedicated each of the four weeks to one of the dogmas of the Blessed Virgin Mary. Since the time of St. De Montfort, the Catholic Church has proclaimed two more *de fide* dogmas on the Blessed Mother. These are the "Immaculate Conception" and the "Assumption of Our Lady body and soul into heaven." The dedication of a dogma for each week, will give an explanation of what each dogma means for further understanding and appreciation of her role in the Church and in our lives.

Finally, I believe that this manual can also be used as a tool for evangelization and catechesis, explaining the role of the Blessed Mother in our lives and how we are to love and honor her as Jesus loved and honored her. Some people today still erroneously think that the Blessed Mother is to be honored in the same way as we honor the angels and the saints. The dogma of the Catholic Church tells us differently. It says that the honor and love that we owe to the Blessed Mother is in a class of its own. To God, the Most Adorable Trinity, alone belongs our adoration and worship. This adoration of the Trinity is called *latriae*. The Church also states that we give veneration or *duliae* to the angels and the saints. The honor and veneration that is due to the Blessed Virgin Mary is substantially less than the adoration that we give to God, yet substantially higher than the veneration that we give to the angels and the saints. The Blessed

Virgin Mary is in a class of her own and the veneration that we owe to her is called *hyperdulia.* The Church puts this forth as a dogma of our faith that is to be believed. To believe otherwise, that is to believe that the Blessed Virgin was just an ordinary person (like any of us) to imitate morally, is to give into the rationalistic and Protestant mentality that is prevalent in the Church today. To our Blessed Mother has been given the power, **by her Son**, to regenerate souls so as to become great saints. Her title is" Queen of all angels and of saints!" No other angel or saint has been given such a title along with its jurisdiction over souls. As St. Maximilian Kolbe states in *Aim Higher* page 14 numbers 9-10, "Through the Immaculate we can become great saints, and what is more, in an easy way. The Immaculate as the Mediatrix of All Graces, not only can and desires to give the grace of conversion and sanctity at certain times and places, but She wants to regenerate *all* souls…."

I believe this manual answers the call of Pope John Paul II's request to, "a renewed understanding of the sacrament of baptism," which would help bring about the "new evangelization." Our Blessed Mother is and has been calling us to consecrate ourselves to Jesus through her, so that she can form us into the likeness of her Son Jesus. When this happens Jesus will then reign in our hearts and the Triumph of the Immaculate Heart of Mary in the world will be manifested.

I pray that all those who read this will increase in their love for Jesus through Mary. I ask that all those who read this will offer a pray for this author that I also will continually increase in my love for Jesus through Mary. May Our Lady find this work pleasing to her and her Son, my Savior Jesus Christ!

How to use this manual

I suggest that each day begin with the prescribed prayers. One may want to start with the Holy Rosary, followed by the daily readings and then finish with the rest of the prayers for the day. Either way, it is good to begin with prayer so as to prepare ones heart for an encounter with Jesus in the Sacred Scriptures. I have arranged the various scriptures readings according to the particular week's theme. For example, the First Period of Twelve Days consists in "casting off the spirit of the world." Therefore, I have used more scripture passages pertinent to casting off the spirit of the world. The numbers in *True Devotion* that follow, relate either to the theme of Sacred Scripture or to the theme of the week. The *Catechism of the Catholic Church* corresponds to the scripture passages of that day. This will greatly enhance ones understanding of the scripture passage and show you how to apply it in our daily life. At the end of each day I have added a quote from various saints and Church Fathers to help drive home the awareness that devotion to Mary can also be found within the Sacred Tradition of the Church. At the end of the thirty-three days you will find instructions from St. De Montfort himself, on how to complete the final day of consecration. Towards the back of the book under the title, "Special Prayers and Practices" are prayers and practices that can be incorporated as part of our interior and exterior practices that will further enhance your love and devotion to the Blessed Mother. It is strongly recommended that this consecration be renewed each year. Therefore, I have put more Feast days for you to choose from, relating to our Blessed Mother, that the Church has added to its calendar since the time of St. Louis De Montfort. I also strongly suggest that after you have made your consecration, that you incorporate into your daily prayer the "Act of Consecration" to Jesus through Mary.

In conclusion, after you have made this act of consecration to Jesus through Mary this should not to be considered as a one-time event, but rather to be taken as a life long commitment. We need a lifetime in order to grow in our love for Jesus through Mary. Let us then ask Jesus to show us His Mother and she in turn will show us Jesus. In order to really understand the sweetness of this devotion, let us begin on our knees, for only in the experience of prayer of the heart will it reveal its treasures.

All for the Immaculata!

Special Feasts for Consecration

Consecration begins on DAY 1 and ends on DAY 33 as follows:
Ending on a special feast day of the Mother of God.

Begin	End	Feast Day
30-Nov	1-Jan	**Mary the Mother of God**
31-Dec	2-Feb	**Purification of the Blessed Mother**
9-Jan	11-Feb	**Our Lady of Lourdes**
20-Feb	25-Mar	**The Annunciation**
26-Mar	28-Apr	**Saint Louis Marie De Montfort**
10-Apr	13-May	**Our Lady of Fatima**
28-Apr	31-May	**Queenship of Mary and Our Lady, Mediatrix of All Graces**
25-May	27-Jun	**Our Lady of Perpetual Help**
13-Jun	16-Jul	**Our Lady of Mount Carmel**
13-Jul	15-Aug	**The Assumption**
20-Jul	22-Aug	**The Immaculate Heart of Mary**
10-Aug	12-Sep	**The Holy Name of Mary**
13-Aug	15-Sep	**The Seven Sorrows of Our Lady**
4-Sep	7-Oct	**The Most Holy Rosary**
25-Oct	27-Nov	**Our Lady of the Miraculous Medal**
5-Nov	8-Dec	**The Immaculate Conception**
9-Nov	12-Dec	**Our Lady of Guadalupe**

TO JESUS THROUGH MARY

First Period Theme

Renouncement of the Spirit of the World

Twelve Preliminary Days

"The first part of the preparation should be employed in casting off the spirit of the world, which is contrary to that of Jesus Christ."

The spirit of the world consists essentially in the denial of the supreme dominion of God, a denial which is manifested in practice by sin and disobedience; thus it is principally opposed to the spirit of Christ, which is also that of Mary.

It manifests itself by the concupiscence of the flesh, by the concupiscence of the eyes and by the pride of life; by disobedience to God's laws and the abuse of created things. Its works are, first, sin in all its forms; and then all else by which the devil leads to sin; works which bring error and darkness to the mind, and seduction and corruption to the will. Its pomps are the splendor and the charms employed by the devil to render sin alluring in persons, places and things.

Daily Prayers during the Twelve Preliminary Days: *Veni Creator, Ave Maris Stella* and the *Holy Rosary.*

Spiritual Exercises during the Twelve Preliminary Days: Examine your conscience, pray (prayer is the lifting up of your mind and heart to God; see also Catechism of the Catholic Church #'s 2673-2682), practice renouncement, mortification (see Catechism of the Catholic

Church #'s 1434-1439), purity of heart; this purity is the indispensable condition for contemplating God in Heaven, seeing Him on earth and knowing Him by the light of Faith (see Catechism of the Catholic Church #'s 2517-2519)

Mary, Mother of God

These twelve preliminary days will be dedicated to Mary under the title "Mother of God" or "*Theotokos*." As you go through the twelve days it would be good to recall the dogma of Mother of God and to invoke her under this title. This is the first *de fide* dogma proclaimed by the Catholic Church at the Council of Ephesus in 431AD. All four dogmas about the Blessed Mother are *de fide*, meaning, they must be believed by all Catholics in order to be catholic. The dogma of Mary, the Mother of God is the foundation of all of her privileges. St. Cyril of Alexandria, who was the official leader at the Council, declared at the Council of Ephesus in 431AD "If any one does not profess that Emmanuel is truly God, and that consequently the Holy virgin is the Mother of God (*Theotokos*), inasmuch as she gave birth in the flesh to the word of God made flesh, let him be anathema."

The dogma, Mother of God contains two truths:

1. Mary truly contributed to the formation of Jesus' human nature, like all mothers do with their children.

2. Mary conceived and bore the Second Person of the Blessed Trinity. This does not mean that she supplied Christ with His divine Person or divine nature, which existed for all eternity.

The Council went on to clarify that because Jesus' human nature is inseparable from His divine Person from the first instant of His conception, than Mary truly conceived and gave birth to a Son who is truly God. A mother cannot be the mother of half the child, but the whole child. Therefore, in the same way Mary cannot be the mother of half of Jesus, but the whole of Jesus. Hence she is really called the Mother of God. For further information see the *Catechism of the Catholic Church # 495*.

Support for this dogma from Sacred Scripture can be found in the Gospel of St. Luke 1:31 and Galatians 4:4.

4

FIRST DAY

Daily Prayers: *Veni Creator, Ave Maris Stella,* the *Holy Rosary.*

Daily Readings: Genesis 3:1-24 and True Devotion #'s 53-54, 45.

Church Teachings For Further Reading: Catechism of the Catholic Church #'s 396-421.

Genesis 3:1-24 Now the serpent was more subtle than any other wild creature that the Lord God had made. He said to the woman, "Did God say, 'You shall not eat of any tree of the garden'?" 2. And the woman said to the serpent, "We may eat of the fruit of the tees of the garden; 3. but God said, 'You shall not eat of the fruit of the tree which is in the midst of the garden, neither shall you touch it, lest you die'." 4. But the serpent said to the woman, "You will not die. 5. For God knows that when you eat of it your eyes will be opened, and you will be like God, knowing good and evil." 6. So when the woman saw that the tree was good for food, and that it was a delight to the eyes, and that the tree was to be desired to make one wise, she took of its fruit and ate; and she also gave some to her husband, and he ate. 7. Then the eyes of both were opened, and they knew that they were naked; and they sewed fig leaves together and made themselves aprons.

8. And they heard the sound of the Lord God walking in the garden in the cool of the day, and the man and his wife hid themselves from the presence of the Lord God among the trees of the garden. 9. But the Lord God called to the man, and said to him, "Where are you?" 10. And he said, "I heard the sound of thee in the

garden, and I was afraid, because I was naked; and I hid myself." 11. He said, "Who told you that you were naked?" 12. The man said, "The woman whom thou gavest to be with me, she gave me fruit of the tree, and I ate." 13. Then the Lord God said to the woman, "What is this that you have done?" The woman said, "The serpent beguiled me, and I ate." 14. The Lord God said to the serpent, "Because you have done this, cursed are you above all cattle, and above all wild animals; upon your belly you shall go, and dust you shall eat all the days of your life. 15. I will put enmity between you and the woman, and between your seed and her seed; he shall bruise your head, and you shall bruise his heel." 16. To the woman he said, "I will greatly multiply your pain in childbearing; in pain you shall bring forth children, yet your desire shall be for your husband, and he shall rule over you." 17. And to Adam he said, "Because you have listened to the voice of your wife, and have eaten of the tree of which I commanded you, 'You shall not eat of it,' cursed is the ground because of you; in toil you shall eat of it all the days of your life; 18. thorns and thistles it shall bring forth to you; and you shall eat the plants of the field. 19. In the sweat of your face you shall eat bread till you return to the ground, for out of it you were taken; you are dust, and to dust you shall return." 20. The man called his wife's name Eve because she was the mother of all the living. 21. And the Lord God made for Adam and for his wife garments of skins, and clothed them. 22. Then the Lord God said, "Behold, the man has become like one of us, knowing good and evil; and now, lest he put forth his hand and take also of the tree of life, and eat, and live for ever" 23. therefore the Lord God sent him forth from the garden of

Eden, to till the ground from which he was taken. 24. He drove out the man; and at the east of the garden of Eden he placed the cherubim, and a flaming sword which turned every way, to guard the way to the tree of life.

True Devotion

#53. What Lucifer lost by pride Mary won by humility. What Eve ruined and lost by disobedience Mary saved by obedience. By obeying the serpent, Eve ruined her children as well as herself and delivered them up to him. Mary, by her perfect fidelity to God, saved her children with herself and consecrated them to his divine majesty.

#54. God has established not just one enmity but "enmities", and not only between Mary and Satan but between her race and his race. That is, God has put enmities, antipathies and hatreds between the true children of the Blessed Virgin and the children and slaves of the devil. They have no love and no sympathy for each other. The children of Belial, the slaves of Satan, the friends of the world - for they are all one and the same - have always persecuted and will persecute more than ever in the future those who belong to the Blessed Virgin, just as Cain of old persecuted his brother Abel, and Esau his brother Jacob. These are the types of the wicked and of the just. But the humble Mary will always triumph over Satan, the proud one, and so great will be her victory that she will crush his head, the very seat of his pride. She will always unmask his serpent's cunning and expose his wicked plots and to the end of time keep her faithful servants from his cruel claws.

But Mary's power over the evil spirits will especially shine forth in the latter times, when Satan will lie in wait for her heel, that is, for her humble servants and her poor children whom she will rouse to fight against him. In the eyes of the world they will be little and poor and, like the heel, lowly in the eyes of all, downtrodden and crushed, as is the heel by the other parts of the body. But in compensation for this they will be rich in God's graces, which will be abundantly bestowed on them by Mary. They will be superior to all creatures by their great zeal and so strongly will they be supported by divine assistance that, in union with Mary, they will crush the head of Satan with their heel, that is, their humility, and bring victory to Jesus Christ.

#45. To Mary alone God gave the keys of the cellars of divine love and the ability to enter the most sublime and secret ways of perfection, and lead others along them. Mary alone gives to the unfortunate children of unfaithful Eve entry into that earthly paradise where they may walk pleasantly with God and be safely hidden from their enemies. There they can feed without fear of death on the delicious fruit of the tree of life and the tree of knowledge of good and evil. They can drink copiously the heavenly waters of that beauteous fountain which gushes forth in such abundance. As she is herself the earthly paradise, that virgin and blessed land from which sinful Adam and Eve were expelled, she lets only those whom she chooses enter her domain in order to make them saints.

"Whoever would say that he does not wish to serve the Mother of God is obedient to the devil, for it is the will of God that we do not lock out the Mother of God."

St. Maximilian Mary Kolbe

SECOND DAY

Daily Prayers: *Veni Creator*, *Ave Maris Stella*, the *Holy Rosary*.
Daily Readings: 1 John 2:15-17; Galatians 5:16-26; Ephesians 2:1-10 and True Devotion #87-89.
Church Teaching For Further Reading: Catechisms of the Catholic Church #'s 377, 2514-2516, 2848, 1470, 2113, 654.

1 John 2:15-17   15. Do not love the world or the things in the world. If any one loves the world, love for the Father is not in him. 16. For all that is in the world, the lust of the flesh and the lust of the eyes and the pride of life, is not of the Father but is of the world. 17. And the world passes away, and the lust of it; but he who does the will of God abides forever.

Galatians 5:16-26   16. But I say, walk by the Spirit, and do not gratify the desires of the flesh. 17. For the desires of the flesh are against the Spirit, and the desires of the Spirit are against the flesh; for these are opposed to each other, to prevent you from doing what you would. 18. But if you are led by the Spirit you are not under the law. 19. Now the works of the flesh are plain: immorality, impurity, licentiousness, 20. idolatry, sorcery, enmity, strife, jealousy, anger, selfishness, dissension, party spirit, 21. envy, drunkenness, carousing, and the like. I warn you, as I warned you before, that those who do such things shall not inherit the kingdom of God. 22. But the fruit of the Spirit is love, joy, peace, patience, kindness, goodness, faithfulness, 23. gentleness, self-control; against such there is no law. 24. And those who belong to Christ Jesus have crucified the flesh with its passions and desires. 25. If we live by the Spirit, let us also walk by the Spirit. 26. Let us have no self-conceit, no provoking of one another, no envy of one another.

Ephesians 2:1-10   And you he made alive, when you were dead through the trespasses and sins 2. in which you once walked, following the course of this world, following the prince of the power of the air, the spirit that is now at work in the sons of disobedience. 3. Among these we all once lived in the passions of our flesh, following the desires of body and mind, and so we were by nature children of wrath, like the rest of mankind. 4. But God, who is rich in mercy, out of the great love with which he loved us, 5. even when were dead through our trespassed, made us alive together with Christ (by grace you have been saved), 6. and raised us up with him, and made us sit with him in the heavenly places in Christ Jesus, 7. that in the coming ages he might show the immeasurable riches of his grace in kindness toward us in Christ Jesus. 8. For by grace you have been saved through faith; and this is not your own doing, it is the gift of God not because of works, lest any man should boast. 10. For we are his workmanship, created in Christ Jesus for good works, which God prepared beforehand, that we should walk in them.

True Devotion

Fifth Principle: It is difficult to keep the graces received from God

#87. It is very difficult, considering our weakness and frailty, to keep the graces and treasures we have received from God. 1. We carry this treasure which is worth more than heaven and earth, in fragile vessels, that is, in a corruptible body and in a weak and wavering soul which requires very little to depress and disturb it.

#88. 2. The evil spirits, cunning thieves that they are, can take us by surprise and rob us of all we posses. They are watching day and night for the right moment. They roam about incessantly seeking to devour us and to snatch from us in one brief moment of sin all the grace and merit we have taken years to acquire. Their malice and their experience, their cunning and their numbers ought to make us ever fearful of such a misfortune happening to us. People richer in grace and virtue, more experienced and advanced in holiness than we are, have been caught off their guard and robbed and stripped of everything. How many cedars of Lebanon, how many stars of the firmament have we sadly watched fall and lose in a short time their loftiness and their brightness!

What has brought about this unexpected reverse? Not the lack of grace, for this is denied no one. It was a lack of humility; they considered themselves well able to hold on to their treasures. They believed their house secure enough and their coffers strong enough to safeguard their precious treasure of grace. It was because of their unconscious reliance on self - although it seemed to them that they were relying solely on the grace of God - that the most just Lord left them to themselves and allowed them to be despoiled. If they had only known of the wonderful devotion that I shall later explain, they would have entrusted their treasure to Mary, the powerful and faithful Virgin. She would have kept it for them as if it were her own possession and even have considered that trust an obligation of justice.

#89. 3. It is difficult to persevere in holiness because of the excessive corrupting influence of the world. The world is so corrupt that it seems almost inevitable that religious hearts be soiled, if not by its mud, at least by its dust. It is something of a miracle for anyone to stand firm in the midst of this raging torrent and not be swept away; to weather this stormy sea and not be drowned, or robbed by pirates; to breathe this pestilential air and not be contaminated by it. It is Mary, the singularly faithful Virgin over whom Satan had never any power, who works this miracle for those who truly lover her.

"When devotion to Mary begins in anyone, it produces the same effect that our Lady's birth produces in the world: it ends the night of sin and leads a person along the bright path of virtue."
St. Alphonsus Liguori

THIRD DAY

Daily Prayers: *Veni Creator, Ave Maris Stella*, the *Holy Rosary.*
Daily Readings: 1 John 1:5-10; 2:1-6 and True Devotion #'s 22-25.
Church Teaching For Further Reading: Catechism of the Catholic Church #'s 2470, 827, 1847.

1 John 1:5-10   5. This is the message we have heard from him and proclaim to you, that God is light and in him is no darkness at all. 6. If we say we have fellowship with him while we walk in darkness, we lie and do not live according to the truth; 7. but if we walk in the light, as he is in the light, we have fellowship with one another, and the blood of Jesus his Son cleanses us from all sin. 8. If we say we have no sin, we deceive ourselves, and the truth is not in us. 9. If we confess our sins, he is faithful and just, and will forgive our sins and cleanse us from all unrighteousness. 10. If we say we have not sinned, we make him a liar, and his word is not in us.

1 John 2:1-6 My little children, I am writing this to you so that you may not sin; but if any one does sin, we have an advocate with the Father, Jesus Christ the righteous; 2. and he is the expiation for our sins, and not for ours only but also for the sins of the whole world. 3. And by this we may be sure that we know him, if we keep his commandments. 4. He who says, "I know him" but disobeys his commandments is a liar, and the truth is not in him; 5. but whoever keeps his word, in him truly love for God is perfected. By this we may be sure that we are in him: 6. he who says he abides in him ought to walk in the same way in which he walked.

True Devotion

2. Mary's part in the sanctification of men

#22. The plan adopted by the three persons of the Blessed Trinity in the Incarnation, the first coming of Jesus Christ, is adhered to each day in an invisible manner throughout the Church and they will pursue it to the end of time until the last coming of Jesus Christ.

#23. God the Father gathered all the waters together and called them the seas or maria. He gathered all his grace together and called it Mary or Maria. The great God has a treasury or storehouse full of riches in which he has enclosed all that is beautiful, resplendent, rare, and precious, even his own Son. This immense treasury is none other than Mary whom the saints call the "treasury of the Lord". From her fullness all men are made rich.

#24. God the Son imparted to his mother all that he gained by his life and death, namely, his infinite merits and his eminent virtues. He made her the treasurer of all his Father had given him as heritage. Through her he applies his merits to his members and through her he transmits his virtues and distributes his graces. She is his mystic channel, his aqueduct, through which he causes his mercies to flow gently and abundantly.

#25. God the Holy Spirit entrusted his wondrous gifts to Mary, his faithful spouse, and chose her as the dispenser of all he

possesses, so that she distributes all his gifts and graces to whom she wills, as much as she will, how she wills and when she wills. No heavenly gift is given to men which does not pass through her virginal hands. Such indeed is the will of God, who has decreed that we should have all things through Mary, so that, making herself poor and lowly, and hiding herself in the depths of nothingness during her whole life, she might thus be enriched, exalted and honored by almighty God. Such are the views of the Church and the early Fathers.

"Do not be afraid, even if you are guilty of every crime possible. Go with trust to this most glorious Lady."
Bernardine deBustis

FOURTH DAY

Daily Prayers: Veni Creator, Ave Maris Stella, the Holy Rosary.

Daily Readings: 1 Peter 4:1-11 and True Devotion #'s 26-28.

Catholic Teaching For Further Reading: Catechism of the Catholic Church #'s 1806, 1434.

1 Peter 4:1-11   Since therefore Christ suffered in the flesh, arm yourselves with the same thought, for whoever has suffered in the flesh has ceased from sin, 2. so as to live for the rest of the time in the flesh no longer by human passions but by the will of God. 3. Let the time that is past suffice for doing what the Gentiles like to do, living in licentiousness, passions, drunkenness, revels, carousing, and lawless idolatry. 4. They are surprised that you do not now join them in the same wild profligacy, and they abuse you; 5. but they will give account to him who is ready to judge the living and the dead. 6. For this is why the gospel was preached even to the dead, that though judged in the flesh like men, they might live in the spirit like God. 7. The end of all things is at hand; therefore keep sane and sober for your prayers. 8. Above all hold unfailing your love for one another, since love covers a multitude of sins.   9. Practice hospitality ungrudgingly to one another. 10. As each has received a gift, employ it for one another, as good stewards of God's varied grace: 11. whoever speaks, as one who utters oracles of God; whoever renders service, as one who renders it by the strength which God supplies; in order that in everything God may be glorified through Jesus Christ. To him belong glory and dominion forever and ever. Amen.

True Devotion

#26. Were I speaking to the so-called intellectuals of today, I would prove at great length by quoting Latin texts taken from Scripture and the Father of the Church all that I am now stating so simply. I could also instance solid proofs which can be read in full in Fr. Poire's book *The Triple Crown of the Blessed Virgin.* But I am speaking mainly for the poor and simple who have more good will and faith than the common run of scholars. As they believe more simply and more meritoriously, let me merely state the truth to them quite plainly without bothering to quote Latin passages which they would not understand. Nevertheless, I shall quote some texts as they occur to my mind as I go along.

#27. Since grace enhances our human nature and glory adds a still greater perfection to grace, it is certain that our Lord remains in heaven just as much the Son of Mary as he was on earth. Consequently he has retained the submissiveness and obedience of the most perfect of all children towards the best of all mothers.

We must take care, however, not to consider this dependence as an abasement or imperfection in Jesus Christ. For Mary, infinitely inferior to her Son, who is God, does not commend him in the same way as an earthly mother would command her child who is beneath her. Since she is completely transformed in God by that grace and glory which transforms all the saints in him, she does not ask or wish or do anything which is contrary to the eternal and unchangeable will of God. When therefore we read in the writings of St. Bernard, St. Bernardine, St. Bonaventure, and others that all in heaven and on earth, even God himself, is subject to the Blessed Virgin, the mean that the authority which God was pleased to give her is so great that she seems to have the same power as God. Her prayers and requests are so powerful with him that he accepts them as commands in the sense that he never resists his dear mother's prayer because it is always humble and conformed to his will.

Moses by the power of his prayer curbed God's anger against the Israelites so effectively that the infinitely great and merciful Lord was unable to withstand him and asked Moses to let him be angry and punish that rebellious people. How much greater, then, will be the prayers and intercession of all the angels and saints in heaven and on earth!

#28. Mary has authority over the angels and the blessed in heaven. As a reward for her great humility, God gave her the power and the mission of assigning to saints the thrones made vacant by the apostate angels who fell away through pride.

Such is the will of almighty God who exalts the humble, that the powers of heaven, earth and hell, willingly or unwillingly, must obey the commands of the humble Virgin Mary. For God has made her queen of heaven and earth, leader of his armies, keeper of his treasures, dispenser of his graces, worker of his wonders, restorer of the human race, mediatrix on behalf of men, destroyer of his enemies, and faithful associate in his great works and triumphs.

"Not sooner had Mary consented to be Mother of the Eternal Word than she merited by this consent to have dominion over the whole word and over every creature."

St. Bernardine of Siena

FIFTH DAY

Daily Prayers: *Veni Creator, Ave Maris Stella*, the *Holy Rosary*.
Daily Readings: James 4:1-17; 5: 1-6 and True Devotion #'s 29-31.
Church Teaching For Further Reading: Catechism of the Catholic Church #'s 2737, 1865, 2409, 2434.

James 4:1-17 What causes wars, and what causes fighting among you? Is it not your passions that are at war in your members? 2. You desire and do not have; so you kill. And you covet and cannot obtain; so you fight and wage war. You do not have, because you do not ask. 3. You ask and do not receive, because you ask wrongly, to spend it on your passions. 4. Unfaithful creatures! Do you not know that friendship with the world is enmity with God? Therefore whoever wishes to be a friend of the world makes himself an enemy of God. 5. Or do you suppose it is in vain that the scripture says, "He yearns jealously over the spirit which he has made to dwell in us?" 6. But he gives more grace; therefore it says, "God opposes the proud, but gives grace to the humble." 7. Submit yourselves therefore to God. Resist the devil and he will flee from you. 8. Draw near to God and he will draw near to you. Cleanse your hands, you sinners, and purify your hearts, you men of double mind. Let your laughter be turned to mourning and your joy to dejection. 10. Humble yourselves before the Lord and he will exalt you. 11. Do not speak evil against one another, brethren. He that speaks evil against a brother or judges his brother, speaks evil against the law and judges the law. But if you judge the law, you are not a doer of the law but a judge, he who is able to save and to destroy. But who are you that you judge your neighbor? 13. Come now, you who say, "Today or tomorrow we will go into such and such a town and spend a year there and trade and get gain"; 14. whereas you do not know about tomorrow. What is your life? For you are a mist that appears for a little time and then vanishes. 15. Instead you ought to say, "If the Lord wills, we shall live and we shall do this or that." 16. As it is, you boast in your arrogance. All such boasting is evil. 17. Whoever knows what is right to do and fails to do to it, for him it is sin.

James 5:1-6 Come now, you rich, weep and howl for the miseries that are coming upon you. 2. Your riches have rotted and your garments are moth-eaten. 3. Your gold and silver have rusted, and their rust will be evidence against you and will eat your flesh like fire. You have laid up treasure for the last days. 4. Behold, the wages of the laborers who mowed your fields, which you kept back by fraud, cry out; and the cries of the harvesters have reached the ears of the Lord of hosts. 5. You have lived on the earth in luxury and in pleasure; you have fattened your hearts in a day of slaughter. 6. You have condemned, you have killed the righteous man; he does not resist you.

True Devotion

#29. God the Father wishes Mary to be the mother of his children until the end of time and so he says to her, "Dwell in Jacob", that is to say, take up your abode permanently in my children, in my

holy ones represented by Jacob, and not in the children of the devil and sinners represented by Esau.

#30. Just as in natural and bodily generation there is a father and a mother, so in the supernatural and spiritual generation there is a father who is God and a mother who is Mary. All true children of God have God for their father and Mary for their mother; anyone who does not have Mary for his mother, does not have God for his father. This is why the reprobate, such as heretics and schismatics, who hate, despise or ignore the Blessed Virgin, do not have God for their father though they arrogantly claim they have, because they do not have Mary for their mother. Indeed if they had her for their mother they would love and honor the mother who gave them life.

#31. God the Son wishes to form himself, and, in a manner of speaking, become incarnate every day in his members through his dear Mother. To her he said, "Take Israel for your inheritance". (Ecclus.24:13) It is as if he said, God the Father has given me as heritage all the nations of the earth, all men good and evil, predestinate and reprobate. To the good I shall be father and advocate, to the bad a just avenger, but to all I shall be a judge. But you, my dear mother, will have for your heritage and possession only the predestinate represented by Israel. As their loving mother, you will give them birth, feed them and rear them. As their queen, you will lead, govern and defend them.

"The Immaculate is the ladder upon which we climb to the Most Sacred Heart of Jesus. Whoever refuses this ladder will not reach the top and will crash to the ground. We strongly believe that She leads us to Jesus…Let whoever teaches otherwise be anathema! Let him be anathema!"

St. Maximilian Mary Kolbe

SIXTH DAY

Daily Prayers: *Veni Creator, Ave Maris Stella*, the *Holy Rosary*.
Daily Readings: Colossians 3:1-11 and True Devotion #'s 32-34.
Church Teaching For Further Reading: Catechism of the Catholic Church #'s 655, 1002, 1420, 2518, 2809.

Colossians 3: 1-11 If then you have been raised with Christ, seek the things that are above, where Christ is, seated at the right hand of God. 2. Set your minds on things that are above, not on things that are on earth. 3. For you have died and your life is hid with Christ in God. 4. When Christ who is our life appears, then you also will appear with him in glory. 5. Put to death therefore what is earthly in you: immorality, impurity, passion, evil desire, and covetousness, which is idolatry. 6. On account of these the wrath of God is coming. 7. In these you once walked, when you lived in them. 8. But now put them all away: anger, wrath, malice, slander, and foul talk from your mouth. 9. Do not lie to one another, seeing that you have put off the old nature with its practices 10. and have put on the new nature, which is being renewed in knowledge after the image of its creator. 11. Here there cannot be Greek and Jew, circumcised and uncircumcised, barbarian, Scythian, slave, free man, but Christ is all, and in all.

True Devotion

#32. "This one and that one were born in her". According to the explanation of some of the Fathers, the first man born of Mary is

the God-man, Jesus Christ. The second is simply man, child of God and Mary by adoption. If Jesus Christ, the head of mankind, is born of her, the predestinate, who are members of this head, must also as a necessary consequence be born of her. One and the same mother does not give birth to the head without the members nor to the members without the head, for these would be monsters in the order of nature. In the order of grace likewise the head and the members are born of the same mother. If a member of the mystical body of Christ, that is, one of the predestinate, were born of a mother other than Mary who gave birth to the head, he would not be one of the predestinate, nor a member of Jesus Christ, but a monster in the order of grace.

#33. Moreover, Jesus is still as much as ever the fruit of Mary, as heaven and earth repeat thousands of times a day, "Blessed is the fruit of thy womb, Jesus." It is therefore certain that Jesus is the fruit and gift of Mary for every single man who possesses him, just as truly as he is for all mankind. Consequently, if any of the faithful have Jesus formed in their heart they can boldly say, "It is thanks to Mary that what I possess is Jesus, her fruit, and without her I would not have him." We can attribute more truly to her what St. Paul said of himself, "I am in labor again with all the children of God until Jesus Christ, my Son, is formed in them to the fullness of his age." St. Augustine, surpassing himself as well as all that I have said so far, affirms that in order to be conformed to the image of the Son of God all the predestinate, while in this world, are hidden in the womb of the Blessed Virgin where they are protected, nourished, cared for and developed by this good Mother, until the day she brings them forth to

a life of glory after death, which the Church calls the birthday of the just. This is indeed a mystery of grace unknown to the reprobate and little known even to the predestinate.

#34. God the Holy Spirit wishes to fashion his chosen ones in and through Mary. He tells her, "My well-beloved, my spouse, let all your virtues take root in my chosen ones that they may grow from strength to strength and from grace to grace. When you were living on earth, practicing the most sublime virtues, I was so pleased with you that I still desire to find you on earth without your ceasing to be in heaven. Reproduce yourself then in my chosen ones, so that I may have the joy of seeing in them the roots of your invincible faith, profound humility, total mortification, sublime prayer, ardent charity, your firm hope and all your virtues. You are always my spouse, as faithful, pure, and fruitful as ever. May your faith give me believers; your purity, virgins; your fruitfulness, elect and living temples."

"The prayers of our Lady, being the prayers of a Mother, have in them something of a command; so it is impossible for her not to be heard."
St. Augustine of Hippo

SEVENTH DAY

Daily Prayers: *Veni Creator, Ave Maris Stella*, the *Holy Rosary*.
Daily Readings: Romans 1:18-32 and True Devotion #'s 35-37.
Church Teaching For Further Reading: Catechism of the Catholic Church #'s 2087, 401, 1777, 2331-2359.

Romans 1:18-32 For the wrath of God is revealed from heaven against all ungodliness and wickedness of men who by their wickedness suppress the truth. 19. For what can be known about God is plain to them, because God has shown it to them. 20. Ever since the creation of the world his invisible nature, namely, his eternal power and deity, has been clearly perceived in the things that have been made. So they are without excuse; 21. for although they knew God they did not honor him as God or give thanks to him, but they became futile in their thinking and their senseless minds were darkened. 22. Claiming to be wise, they became fools, 23. and exchanged the glory of the immortal God for images resembling mortal man or birds or animals or reptiles. 24. Therefore God gave them up in the lusts of their hearts to impurity, to the dishonoring of their bodies among themselves, 25. because they exchanged the truth about God for a lie and worshipped and served the creature rather than the Creator, who is blessed forever! Amen. 26. For this reason God gave them up to dishonorable passions. Their women exchanged natural relations for unnatural, 27. and the men likewise gave up natural relations with women and were consumed with passion for one another, men committing shameless acts with men and receiving in their own persons the due penalty for their error. 28. And since they did not see fit to acknowledge God, God gave them up to a base mind and to improper conduct. 29. They were filled with all manner of wickedness, evil, covetousness, malice. Full of envy, murder, strife, deceit, malignity, they are gossips, 30. slanderers, haters of God, insolent, haughty, boastful, inventors of evil, disobedient to parents, 31. foolish, faithless, heartless, ruthless. 32. Though they know God's decree that those who do such things deserve to die, they not only do them but approve those who practice them.

True Devotion

#35. When Mary has taken root in a soul she produces in it wonders of grace which only she can produce; for she alone is the fruitful virgin who never had and never will have her equal in purity and fruitfulness. Together with the Holy Spirit Mary produced the greatest thing that ever was or ever will be: a God-man. She will consequently produce the marvels which will be seen in the latter times. The formation and the education of the great saints who will come at the end of the world are reserved to her, for only this singular and wondrous virgin can produce in union with the Holy Spirit singular and wondrous things.

#36. When the Holy Spirit, her spouse, finds Mary in a soul, he hastens there and enters fully into it. He gives himself generously to that soul according to the place it has given to his spouse. One of the main reasons why the Holy Spirit does not now work striking wonders in souls is that he fails to find in them a sufficiently close

union with his faithful and inseparable spouse. I say "inseparable spouse", for from the moment the substantial love of the Father and the Son espoused Mary to form Jesus, the head of the elect, and Jesus in the elect, he has never disowned her, for she has always been faithful and fruitful.

3. Consequences

#37. We must obviously conclude from what I have just said:

First, that Mary has received from God a far-reaching dominion over the souls of the elect. Otherwise she could not make her dwelling-place in them as God the Father has ordered her to do, and she could not conceive them, nourish them, and bring them forth to eternal life as their mother. She could not have them for her inheritance and her possession and form them in Jesus and Jesus in them. She could not implant in their heart the roots of her virtues, nor be the inseparable associate of the Holy Spirit in all these works of grace. None of these things, I repeat, could she do unless she had received from the Almighty rights and authority over their souls. For God, having given her power over his only-begotten and natural Son, also gave her power over his adopted children, not only in what concerns their body - which would be of little account - but also in what concerns their souls.

"The Holy Ghost does not act, except through the Immaculate His Spouse. Hence She is the Mediatrix of all the graces of the Most Holy Ghost."

St. Maximilian Mary Kolbe

EIGHTH DAY

Daily Prayers: *Veni Creator, Ave Maris Stella*, the *Holy Rosary*.

Daily Readings: Romans 6:1-14 and True Devotion #'s 38-40.

Church Teaching For Further Reading: Catechism of the Catholic Church #'s 1006, 1214, 1227, 1987, 790, 1694, 2819.

Romans 6:1-14 What shall we say then? Are we to continue in sin that grace may abound? 2. By no means! How can we who died to sin still live in it? 3. Do you not know that all of us who have been baptized into Christ Jesus were baptized into his death? 4. We were buried therefore with him by baptism into death, so that as Christ was raised from the dead by the glory of the Father, we too might walk in newness of life. 5. For if we have been united with him in a death like his, we shall certainly be united with him in a resurrection like his. 6. We know that our old self was crucified with him so that the sinful body might be destroyed, and we might no longer be enslaved to sin. 7. For he who has died is freed from sin. 8. But if we have died with Christ, we believed that we shall also live with him. 9. For we know that Christ being raised from the dead will never die again; death no longer has dominion over him. 10. The death he died he died to sin, once for all, but the life he lives he lives to God. 11. So you also must consider yourselves dead to sin and alive to God in Christ Jesus. 12. Let not sin therefore reign in your mortal bodies, to make you obey their passions. 13. Do not yield your members to sin as instruments of wickedness, but yield yourselves to God as men who have been brought from death to life, and your members to God as instruments of righteousness. 14. For sin will have no dominion over you, since you are not under law but under grace.

True Devotion

#38. Mary is the Queen of heaven and earth by grace as Jesus is King by nature and by conquest. But as the kingdom of Jesus Christ exists primarily in the heart or interior of man, according to the words of the Gospel, "The kingdom of God is within you", so the kingdom of the Blessed Virgin is principally in the interior of man, that is, in his soul. It is principally in souls that she is glorified with her Son more than in any visible creatures. So we may call her, as the saints do, *Queen of our hearts.*

#39. Secondly, we must conclude that, being necessary to God by a necessity which is called 'hypothetical', (that is, because God so willed it), the Blessed Virgin is all the more necessary for men to attain their final end. Consequently we must not place devotion to her on the same level as devotion to the other saints as if it were merely something optional.

#40. The pious and learned Jesuit, Suarez, Justus Lipsuis, a devout and erudite theologian of Louvain, and many others have proved incontestably that devotion to our Blessed Lady is necessary to attain salvation. This they show from the teaching of the Fathers, notably St. Augustine, St. Ephrem, deacon of Edessa, St. Cyril of Jerusalem, St. Germanus of Constantinople, St. John Damascene, St. Anselm, St. Bernard, St. Bernardine, St. Thomas and St. Bonaventure. Even according to Aescalampadius and other heretics, lack of esteem and love for the Virgin Mary is an infallible sign of

God's disapproval. On the other hand, to be entirely and genuinely devoted to her is a sign of God's approval.

"Among the Saints,
we do not make use of one to intercede with the other,
because they are all of the same order.
But we do ask them to intercede with Mary,
because she is their Sovereign and Queen."

Francis Suarez

NINTH DAY

Daily Prayers: *Veni Creator, Ave Maris Stella,* the *Holy Rosary.*
Daily Readings: Ephesians 5:1-20 and True Devotion #'s 41-43.
Church Teaching For Further Reading: Catechism of the Catholic Church #'s 2113, 1695.

Ephesians 5:1-20   Therefore be imitators of God, as beloved children. 2. And walk in love, as Christ loved us and gave himself up for us, a fragrant offering and sacrifice to God.

   3. But immorality and all impurity or covetousness must not even be named among you, as is fitting among saints. 4. Let there be no filthiness, nor silly talk, nor levity, which are not fitting; but instead let there be thanksgiving. 5. Be sure of this, that no immoral or impure man, or one who is covetous (that is, an idolater), has any inheritance in the kingdom of Christ and of God. 6. Let no one deceive you with empty words, for it is because of these things that the wrath of God comes upon the sons of disobedience. 7. Therefore do not associate with them, for once you were darkness, but now you are light in the Lord; walk as children of light 9.(for the fruit of light is found in all that is good and right and true), 10. and try to learn what is pleasing to the Lord. 11. Take no part in the unfruitful works of darkness, but instead expose them. 12. For it is a shame even to speak of the things that they do in secret; 13. but when anything is exposed by the light it becomes visible, for anything that becomes visible is light. 14. Therefore it is said, "Awake, O sleeper, and arise from the dead, and Christ shall give you light."

15. Look carefully then how you walk, not as unwise men but as wise, 16. making the most of the time, because the days are evil. 17. Therefore do not be foolish, but understand what the will of the Lord is. 18. And do not get drunk with wine, for that is debauchery; but be filled with the Spirit, 19. addressing one another in psalms and hymns and melody to the Lord with all your heart, 20. always and for everything giving thanks in the name of our Lord Jesus Christ to God the Father.

True Devotion

#41. The types and texts of the Old and New Testament prove the truth of this, the opinions and examples of the saints confirm it, and reason and experience teach and demonstrate it. Even the devil and his followers, forced by the evidence of the truth, were frequently obliged against their will to admit it. For brevity's sake, I shall quote one only of the many passages which I have collected from the Fathers and Doctors of the Church to support this truth. "Devotion to you, O Blessed Virgin, is a means of salvation which God gives to those whom he wishes to save" (St. John Damascene).

#42. I could tell many stories in evidence of what I have just said.

1. One is recorded in the chronicles of St. Francis. The saint saw in ecstasy an immense ladder reaching to heaven, at the top of which stood the Blessed Virgin. This is the ladder, he was told, by which we must all go to heaven.

2. There is another related in the Chronicles of St. Dominic. Near Carcassonne, where St. Dominic was preaching the Rosary,

there was an unfortunate heretic who was possessed by a multitude of devils. These evil spirits to their confusion were compelled at the command of our Lady to confess many great and consoling truths concerning devotion to her. They did so clearly and forcibly that, however weak our devotion to our Lady may be, we cannot read this authentic story containing such an unwilling tribute paid by the devils to devotion to our Lady without shedding tears of joy.

#43. If devotion to the Blessed Virgin is necessary for all men simply to work out their salvation, it is even more necessary for those who are called to a special perfection. I do not believe that anyone can acquire intimate union with our Lord and perfect fidelity to the Holy Spirit without a very close union with the most Blessed Virgin and an absolute dependence on her support.

"The rosary shall be a powerful armour against hell, it will destroy vice, decrease sin, and defeat heresies."
St. Dominic

TENTH DAY

Daily Prayers: *Veni Creator, Ave Maris Stella,* the *Holy Rosary.*

Daily Readings: 2 Timothy 3:1-9 and True Devotion #'s 44, 45, 46, 48.

Church Teaching For Further Reading: Catechism of the Catholic Church #'s 1852-1864.

2 Timothy 3: 1-9 But understand this, that in the last days there will come times of stress. 2. For men will be lovers of self, lovers of money, proud, arrogant, abusive, disobedient to their parents, ungrateful, unholy, 3. inhuman, implacable, slanderers, profligates, fierce, haters of good, 4. treacherous, reckless, swollen with conceit, lovers of pleasure rather than lovers of God, 5. holding to the form of religion but denying the power of it. Avoid such people. 6. For among them are those who make their way into households and capture weak women, burdened with sins and swayed by various impulses, 7. who will listen to anybody and can never arrive at a knowledge of the truth. 8. As Jannes and Jambres opposed Moses, so these men also oppose the truth, men of corrupt mind and counterfeit faith; 9. but they will not get very far, for their folly will be plain to all, as was that of those two men.

True Devotion

#44. Mary alone found grace before God without the help of any other creature. All those who have since found grace before God have found it only through her. She was full of grace when she was

greeted by the Archangel Gabriel and was filled with grace to overflowing by the Holy Spirit when he so mysteriously overshadowed her. From day to day, from moment to moment she increased so much this twofold plenitude that she attained an immense and inconceivable degree of grace. So much so, that the Almighty made her the sole custodian of his treasures and the sole dispenser of his graces. She can lead them along the narrow path to heaven and guide them through the narrow gate to life. She can give a royal throne, sceptre and crown to whom she wishes. Jesus is always and everywhere the fruit and Son of Mary and Mary is everywhere the genuine tree that bears that Fruit of life, the true Mother who bears that Son.

#45. To Mary alone God gave the keys of the cellars of divine love and the ability to enter the most sublime and secret ways of perfection, and lead others along them. Mary alone gives to the unfortunate children of unfaithful Eve entry into that earthly paradise where they may walk pleasantly with God and be safely hidden from their enemies. There they can feed without fear of death on the delicious fruit of the tree of life and that tree of knowledge of good and evil. They can drink copiously the heavenly waters of that beauteous fountain which gushes forth in such abundance. As she is herself the earthly paradise, that virgin and blessed land from which sinful Adam and Eve were expelled, she lets only those whom she chooses enter her domain in order to make them saints.

#46. All the rich among the people, to use an expression of the Holy Spirit as explained by St. Bernard, all the rich among the people will look pleadingly upon your countenance throughout all

ages and particularly as the world draws to its end. This means that the greatest saints, those richest in grace and virtue, will be the most assiduous in praying to the most Blessed Virgin, looking up to her as the perfect model to imitate and as a powerful helper to assist them.

#48. These souls filled with grace and zeal will be chosen to oppose the enemies of God who are raging on all sides. They will be exceptionally devoted to the Blessed Virgin. Illumined by her light, strengthened by her food, guided by her spirit, supported by her arm, sheltered under her protection, they will fight with one hand and build with the other (Nehem.4:17). With one hand they will give battle, overthrowing and crushing heretics and their heresies, schismatics and their schisms, idolaters and their idolatries, sinners and their wickedness. With the other hand they will build the temple of the true Solomon and the mystical city of God, namely, the Blessed Virgin, who is called by the Fathers of the Church the *Temple of Solomon* and the *City of God (Ps. 86:3)*. By word and example they will draw all men to a true devotion to her and though this will make them many enemies, it will also bring about many victories and much glory to God alone. This is what God revealed to St. Vincent Ferrer, that outstanding apostle of his day, as he has amply shown in one of his works.

This seems to have been foretold by the Holy Spirit in Psalm 58 "The Lord will reign in Jacob and all the ends of the earth. They will be converted towards evening and they will be as hungry as dogs and they will go around the city to find something to eat." This city around which men will roam at the end of the world seeking conversion and the appeasement of the hunger they have for justice is the Blessed Virgin, who is called by the Holy Spirit the *City of God*.

"The rosary is the scourge of the devil"
Pope Adrian VI

ELEVENTH DAY

Daily Prayers: *Veni Creator, Ave Maris Stella*, the *Holy Rosary*.

Daily Readings: Gospel of St. Matthew 3:1-17 and True Devotion #'s 126-130.

Church Teaching For Further Reading: Catechism of the Catholic Church #'s 523, 535-537, 541.

Gospel of St. Matthew 3:1-17 In those days came John the Baptist, preaching in the wilderness of Judea. 2. "Repent, for the kingdom of heaven is at hand." 3. For this is he who was spoken of by the prophet Isaiah when he said, "The voice of one crying in the wilderness: Prepare the way of the Lord, make his paths straight." 4. Now John wore a garment of camel's hair, and a leather girdle around his waist; and his food was locust and wild honey. 5. Then went out to him Jerusalem and all Judea and all the region about the Jordan, 6. and they were baptized by him in the river Jordan, confessing their sins.

7. But when he saw many of the Pharisees and Sadducees coming for baptism, he said to them, "You brood of vipers! Who warned you to flee from the wrath to come? Bear fruit that befits repentance, 9. and do not presume to say to yourselves, 'We have Abraham as our father'; for I tell you, God is able from these stones to raise up children to Abraham. 10. Even now the axe is laid to the root of the trees; every tree therefore that does not bear good fruit is cut down and thrown into the fire.

11. "I baptize you with water for repentance, but he who is coming after me is mightier than I, whose sandals I am not worthy to carry; he will baptize you with the Holy Spirit and with fire. 12. His winnowing fork is in his hand, and he will clear his threshing floor and gather his wheat into the granary, but the chaff he will burn with unquenchable fire."

13. Then Jesus came from Galilee to the Jordan to John, to be baptized by him. 14. John would have prevented him saying, "I need to be baptized by you, and do you come to me?" 15. But Jesus answered him, *"Let it be so now; for thus it is fitting for us to fulfill all righteousness."* Then he consented. 16. And when Jesus was baptized, he went up immediately from the water, and behold, the heavens were opened and he saw the Spirit of God descending like a dove, and alighting on him; 17. and lo, a voice from heaven, saying, *"This is my beloved Son, with whom I am well pleased."*

True Devotion

2. A perfect renewal of baptismal promises

#126. I have said that this devotion could rightly be called a perfect renewal of the vows and promises of holy baptism. Before baptism every Christian was a slave of the devil because he belonged to him. At baptism he has either personally or through his sponsors solemnly renounced Satan, his seductions and his works. He has chosen Jesus as his Master and sovereign Lord and undertaken to depend upon him as a slave of love. This is what is done in the

devotion I am presenting to you. We renounce the devil, the world, sin and self, as expressed in the act of consecration, and we give ourselves entirely to Jesus through Mary. We even do something more than at baptism, when ordinarily our god-parents speak for us and we are given to Jesus only by proxy. In this devotion we give ourselves personally and freely and we are fully aware of what we are doing.

In holy baptism we do not give ourselves to Jesus explicitly through Mary, nor do we give him the value of our good actions. After baptism we remain entirely free either to apply that value to anyone we wish or keep it for ourselves. But by this consecration we give ourselves explicitly to Jesus through Mary's hands and we include in our consecration the value of all our actions.

#127. "Men" says St. Thomas, "vow in baptism to renounce the devil and all his seductions." "This vow," says St. Augustine, "is the greatest and the most indispensable of all vows." Canon Law experts say the same thing: "The vow we make at baptism is the most important of all vows." But does anyone keep this great vow? Does anyone fulfill the promises of baptism faithfully? Is it not true that nearly all Christians prove unfaithful to the promises made to Jesus in baptism? Where does this universal failure come from, if not from man's habitual forgetfulness of the promises and responsibilities of baptism and from the fact that scarcely anyone makes a personal ratification of the contract made with God through his sponsors?

#128. This is so true that the Council of Sens, convened by order of the Emperor Louis the Debonair to remedy the grave disorders of Christendom, came to the conclusion that the main cause

of this moral breakdown was man's forgetfulness of his baptismal obligations and his disregard for them. It could suggest no better way of remedying this great evil than to encourage all Christians to renew the promises and vows of baptism.

#129. The *Catechism of the Council of Trent,* the faithful interpreter of that holy Council, exhorts the parish priests to do the same thing, and to induce the people to remind themselves, and to believe, that they are bound and consecrated as slaves to Our Lord Jesus Christ, their Redeemer and their Lord. These are its words: "The parish priest shall exhort the faithful people so that they may know that it is most just... that we should devote and consecrate ourselves forever to our Redeemer and Lord as His very slaves."

#130. Now the Councils, the Fathers of the Church and experience itself, all indicate that the best remedy for the frequent lapses of Christians is to remind them of the responsibilities of their baptism and have them renew the vows they made at that time. Is it not reasonable therefore to do this in our day and in a perfect manner by adopting this devotion with its consecration to our Lord through his Blessed Mother? I say, "in a perfect manner," for in making this consecration to Jesus we are adopting the perfect means of giving ourselves to him, which is the most Blessed Virgin Mary.

"God will not save us without the intercession of Mary"
St. Bonaventure

TWELFTH DAY

Daily Prayers: *Veni Creator, Ave Maris Stella*, the *Holy Rosary.*
Daily Readings: Gospel of St. John 3:1-21 and True Devotion #'s 131-133.
Church Teaching For Further Reading: Catechism of the Catholic Church #'s 215, 1225, 1238, 1257, 1262, 526, 591, 505, 2130, 219, 454, 679.

Gospel of St. John 3:1-21 Now there was a man of the Pharisees, named Nicodemus, a ruler of the Jews. 2. This man came to Jesus by night and said to him, "Rabbi, we know that you are a teacher come from God; for no one can do these signs that you do, unless God is with him." 3. Jesus answered him, *"Truly, truly, I say to you, unless one is born anew, he cannot see the kingdom of God."* 4. Nicodemus said to him, "How can a man be born when he is old? Can a man be born when he is old? Can he enter a second time into his mother's womb and be born? 5. Jesus answered, *"Truly, truly, I say to you, unless one is born of water and the Spirit, he cannot enter the kingdom of God. 6. That which is born of the flesh is flesh, and that which is born of the Spirit is spirit. 7. Do not marvel that I said to you, 'You must be born anew.' 8. The wind blows where it wills, and you hear the sound of it, but you do not know whence it comes or whither it goes; so it is with every one who is born of the Spirit."* 9. Nicodemus said to him, "How can this be?" 10. Jesus answered him, *"Are you a teacher of Israel, and yet you do not understand this? 11. Truly, truly, I say to you, we speak of what we know, and bear* *witness to what we have seen; but you do not receive our testimony. 12 If I have told you earthly things and you do not believe, how can you believe if I tell you heavenly things? 13. No one has ascended into heaven but he who descended from heaven, the Son of man. 14. And as Moses lifted up the serpent in the wilderness, so must the Son of man be lifted up, 15. that whoever believes in him may have eternal life." 16. For God so loved the world that he gave his only Son, that whoever believes in him should not perish but have eternal life. 17. For God sent the Son into the world, not to condemn the world, but that the world might be saved through him. 18. He who believes in him is not condemned; he who does not believe is condemned already, because he has not believed in the name of the only Son of God. 19. And this is the judgment, that the light has come into the world, and men loved darkness rather than light, because their deeds were evil. 20. For every one who does evil hates the light, and does not come to the light, lest his deeds should be exposed. 21. But he who does what is true comes to the light, that it may be clearly seen that his deeds have been wrought in God."*

True Devotion

#131. No one can object that this devotion is novel or of no value. It is not new, since the Councils, the Fathers of the Church, and many authors both past and present, speak of consecration to our Lord or renewal of baptismal vows as something going back to ancient times and recommended to all the faithful. Nor is it valueless, since the chief source of moral disorders and the

consequent eternal loss of Christians spring from forgetfulness of this practice and indifference to it.

#132. Some may object that this devotion makes us powerless to help the souls of our relatives, friends and benefactors, since it requires us to give our Lord, through Mary, the value of our good works, prayers, penances, and alms-giving.

To them I reply: 1) It is inconceivable that our friends, relatives and benefactors should suffer any loss because we have dedicated and consecrated ourselves unconditionally to the service of Jesus and Mary; it would be an affront to the power and goodness of Jesus and Mary who will surely come to the aid of our relatives, friends and benefactors whether from our meager spiritual assets or from other sources.

2) This devotion does not prevent us from praying for others, both the living and the dead, even though the application of our good works depends on the will of our Blessed Lady. On the contrary, it will make us pray with even greater confidence. Imagine a rich man, who, wanting to show his esteem for a great prince, gives his entire fortune to him. Would not that man have greater confidence in asking the prince to help one of his friends who needs assistance? Indeed the prince would only be too happy to have such an opportunity of proving his gratitude to one who had sacrificed all that he possessed to enrich him, thereby impoverishing himself to do him honor. The same must be said of our Lord and our Lady. They will never allow themselves to be outdone in gratitude.

#133. Some may say, perhaps, if I give our Lady the full value of my actions to apply it to whom she wills, I may have to suffer a long

time in purgatory. This objection, which arises from self-love and from an unawareness of the generosity of God and his holy Mother, refutes itself.

Take a fervent and generous soul who values God's interests more than his own. He gives God all he has without reserve till he can give no more. He desires only that the glory and the kingdom of Jesus may come about. Will this generous and unselfish soul, I ask, be punished more in the next world for having been more generous and unselfish than other people? Far from it! For we shall see later that our Lord and his Mother will prove most generous to such a soul with gifts of nature, grace and glory in this life and in the next.

"The more we belong to the Immaculate, the more perfectly will we understand the love of Jesus, God the Father, and the Most Blessed Trinity."

St. Maximilian Mary Kolbe

Second Period Theme
Knowledge of Self

Next Seven Days

During the first week you should offer up all your prayers and pious actions to ask for a knowledge of yourself and contrition for your sin; and you should do this in a spirit of humility. You can look upon yourself during the six days of this week as a snail, crawling things, a toad, a swine, a serpent and unclean animals; or you can reflect on these three considerations of Saint Bernard: the vileness of your origin, the dishonor of your present state, and your ending as the food of worms. You should pray that Our Lord and the Holy Ghost enlighten you; and for that end you might use the ejaculations, "Lord, that I may see!;" or "May I know myself!;" or "Come, Holy Ghost," together with the Litany of the Holy Ghost. You should have recourse to the Blessed Virgin and ask her to grant you this immense grace, which must be the foundation of all others.

During this week, consider not so much the opposition that exists between the spirit of Jesus and you, as the miserable and humiliating state to which your sins have reduced you. Moreover, the True Devotion being as easy, short, sure and perfect way to arrive at that union with Our Lord which is Christian perfection, you should enter seriously upon this way, strongly convinced of your misery and helplessness. But how can you attain this without a knowledge of yourself?

Daily Prayers: *Litany of the Holy Ghost,* the *Ave Maris Stella,* and the *Holy Rosary.*

Spiritual Exercises: Prayers, examens, reflection, acts of renouncement of your will, of contrition for your sins, of contempt of self-all performed at the feet of Mary, for it is from her you hope for light to know yourself, and it is near her that you shall be able to measure the abyss of your miseries without despairing.

Mary, Perpetual Virgin

These next seven days, Knowledge of Self, will be dedicated to the *de fide* dogma of Mary's Perpetual Virginity. This dogma was proclaimed at the Council of Lateran in 649AD. It proclaimed that Mary was a virgin before, during and after she gave birth to Jesus and that her bodily integrity was kept intact.

Pope St. Martin I, declared this dogma by stating, "If anyone does not, in accord with the holy Fathers, acknowledge the holy, ever virgin and immaculate Mary as really and truly the Mother of God, inasmuch as she, in the fullness the time, and without seed, conceived by the Holy Spirit of God the Word Himself, who before all time was born of God the Father, and without loss of integrity brought Him forth, and after His birth preserved her virginity inviolate, let him be condemned."

Mary was a virgin before the birth of Jesus because she conceived Jesus by the power of the Holy Spirit without the cooperation of man. Mary was a virgin during the birth of Jesus, by the fact that Jesus left Mary's womb in a miraculous manner, that is to say without opening the womb or any other part of Mary's body. Jesus passed through Mary's womb like light passes through glass.

Mary was a virgin after the birth of Jesus, meaning that she did not have any children after Jesus was born. She did not have any relations with man, not even with St. Joseph. Finally, Mary remained a virgin unto death. For further reading on this subject read the Catechism of the Catholic Church #'s 499-507.

Support for this dogma of Mary's Perpetual Virginity can be found in Isaiah 7:14; Luke 1:26-38; Luke 2:5.

THIRTEENTH DAY

Daily Prayers: *Litany of the Holy Ghost,* the *Ave Maris Stella,* and the *Holy Rosary.*

Daily Readings: Matthew 5:1-43 and True Devotion # 78.

Church Teaching For Further Reading: Catechism of the Catholic Church #'s 1965-68, 1831, 544, 2546, 2447, 2517-19, 2305, 577-81, 1963-68, 2302, 1034-35, 2380, 2382, 2153-54, 1933, 2842.

Gospel of St. Matthew 5:1-43 Seeing the crowds, he went up on the mountain, and when he sat down his disciples came to him. 2. And he opened his mouth and taught them, saying:

3. "Blessed are the poor in spirit, for theirs is the kingdom of heaven. 4. Blessed are those who mourn, for they shall be comforted. 5. Blessed are the meek, for they shall inherit the earth. 6. Blessed are those who hunger and thirst for righteousness, for they shall be satisfied. 7. Blessed are the merciful, for they shall obtain mercy. 8. Blessed are the pure in heart, for they shall see God. 9. Blessed are the peacemakers, for they shall be called sons of God. 10. Blessed are those who are persecuted for righteousness' sake, for theirs is the kingdom of heaven. 11. Blessed are you when men revile you and persecute you and utter all kinds of evil against you falsely on my account. 12. Rejoice and be glad, for your reward is great in heaven, for so men persecuted the prophets who were before you.

13. You are the salt of the earth; but if salt has lost its taste, how shall its saltness be restored? It is no longer good for anything except to be thrown out and trodden under foot by men.

14. You are the light of the world. A city set on a hill cannot be hid. 15. Nor do men light a lamp and put it under a bushel, but on a stand, and it gives light to all in the house. 16. Let your light so shine before men, that they may see your good works and give glory to your Father who is in heaven.

17. Think not that I have come to abolish the law and the prophets; I have come not to abolish them but to fulfill them. 18. For truly, I say to you, till heaven and earth pass away, not an iota, not a dot, will pass from the law until all is accomplished. 19. Whoever then relaxes one of the least of these commandments and teaches men so, shall be called least in the kingdom of heaven; but he who does them and teaches them shall be called great in the kingdom of heaven. 20. For I tell you, unless your righteousness exceeds that of the scribes and Pharisees, you will never enter the kingdom of heaven. 21. But I say to you that every one who is angry with his brother shall be liable to judgment; whoever insults his brother shall be liable to the council, and whoever says, 'You fool!' shall be liable to the hell of fire. 23. So if you are offering your gift and your brother has something against you, 24. leave your gift there before the altar and go; first be reconciled to your brother, and then come and offer your gift. 25. Make friends quickly with your accuser, while you are going with him to court, lest your accuser hand you over to the judge, and the judge to the guard, and you be put in prison; 26. truly, I say to you, you will never get out till you have paid the last penny.

27. You have heard that it was said, 'You shall not commit adultery.' 28. But I say to you that every one who looks at a woman

lustfully has already committed adultery with her in his heart. 29. *If your right eye causes you to sin, pluck it out and throw it away; it is better that you lose one of your members than that your whole body be thrown into hell.* 30. *And if your right hand causes you to sin, cut it off and throw it away; it is better that you lose one of your members than that your whole body go into hell.*

31. *It was also said, 'Whoever divorces his wife, let him give her a certificate of divorce.'* 32. *But I say to you that every one who divorces his wife, except on the ground of unchastity, makes her an adulteress; and whoever marries a divorced woman commits adultery.*

33. *Again you have heard that it was said to the men of old, 'You shall not swear falsely, but shall perform to the Lord what you have sworn.'* 34. *But I say to you, Do not swear at all, either by heaven, for it is the throne of God,* 35. *or by the earth, for it is his footstool, or by Jerusalem, for it is the city of the great King.* 36. *And do not swear by your head, for you cannot make one hair white or black.* 37. *Let what you say be simply 'Yes' or 'No'; anything more than this comes from evil.*

38. *You have heard that it was said, 'An eye for an eye and a tooth for a tooth.'* 39. *But I say to you, Do not resist one who is evil. But if any one strikes you on the right cheek, turn to him the other also;* 40. *and if any one would sue you and take your coat, let him have your cloak as well;* 41. *and if any one forces you to go one mile, go with him two miles.* 42. *Give to him who begs from you, and do not refuse him who would borrow from you."*

True Devotion

Third Principle: We must rid ourselves of what is evil in us

#78   Our best actions are usually tainted and spoiled by the evil that is rooted in us. When pure, clear water is poured into a foul-smelling jug, or wine into an unwashed cask that previously contained another wine, the clear water and the good wine are tainted and readily acquire an unpleasant odor. In the same way when God pours into our souls, infected by original and actual sin, the heavenly waters of his grace or the delicious wines of his love, his gifts are usually spoiled and tainted by the evil sediment left in us by sin. Our actions, even those of the highest virtue, show the effects of it. It is therefore of the utmost importance that, in seeking the perfection that can be attained only by union with Jesus, we rid ourselves of all that is evil in us. Otherwise our infinitely pure Lord, who has a infinite hatred for the slightest stain in our soul, will refuse to unite us to himself and will drive us from his presence.

"When a soul in sin begins to show signs of devotion to Mary,
it is a clear indication that before very long
God will enrich it with His grace."
St. Alphonsus Liguori

FOURTEENTH DAY

Daily Prayers: Litany of the Holy Ghost, Ave Maris Stella, and the Holy Rosary.

Daily Readings: Gospel of St. Matthew 6:1-34 and True Devotion #'s 79-80.

Church Teaching For Further Reading: Catechism of the Catholic Church #'s 1434, 1969, 1430, 2447, 2602, 2655, 2668, 2768, 2766, 2780, 2807, 2837, 1438, 2113, 2830, 2608.

Gospel of St. Matthew 6: 1-34 *"Beware of practicing your piety before men in order to be seen by them; for then you will have no reward from your Father who is in heaven.*

2. Thus, when you give alms, sound no trumpet before you, as the hypocrites do in the synagogues and in the streets, that they may be praised by men. Truly, I say to you, they have their reward. 3. But when you give alms, do not let your left hand know what your right hand is doing, 4. so that your alms may be in secret; and your Father who sees in secret will reward you.

5. And when you pray, you must not be like the hypocrites; for they love to stand and pray in the synagogues and at the street corners, that they may be seen by men. Truly, I say to you, they have their reward. 6. But when you pray, go into your room and shut the door and pray to your Father who is in secret; and your Father who sees in secret will reward you.

7. And in praying do not heap up empty phrases as the Gentiles do; for they think that they will be heard for their many words. 8. Do not be like them, for your Father knows what you need before you ask him. 9. Pray then like this: Our Father who art in heaven, Hallowed be thy name. Thy kingdom come, Thy will be done, on earth as it is in heaven. Give us this day our daily bread; and forgive us our debts, as we also have forgiven our debtors; and lead us not into temptation, but deliver us from evil. 14. For if you forgive men their trespasses, your heavenly Father also will forgive you; 15. but if you do not forgive men their trespasses, neither will your Father forgive your trespasses.

16. And when you fast, do not look dismal, like the hypocrites, for they disfigure their faces that their fasting may be seen by men. Truly, I say to you, they have their reward. 17. But when you fast, anoint your head and wash your face, 18. that your fasting may not be seen by men but by your Father who is in secret; and your Father who sees in secret will reward you.

19. Do not lay up for yourselves treasures on earth, where moth and rust consume and where thieves break in and steal, 20. but lay up for yourselves treasures in heaven, where neither moth nor rust consumes and where thieves do not break in and steal. 21. For where your treasure is, there will your heart be also.

22. The eye is the lamp of the body. So, if your eye is sound, your whole body will be full of light; 23. but if your eye is not sound, your whole body will be full of darkness. If then the light in you is darkness, how great is the darkness!

24. No one can serve two masters; for either he will hate the one and love the other, or he will be devoted to the one and despise the other. You cannot serve God and mammon.

25. Therefore I tell you, do not be anxious about your life, what you shall eat or what you shall drink, nor about your body, what you shall put on. Is not life more than food, and the body more than clothing? 26. Look at the birds of the air; they neither sow nor reap nor gather into barns, and yet your heavenly Father feeds them. Are you not of more value than they? 27. And which of you by being anxious can add one cubit to his span of life? 28. And why are you anxious about clothing? Consider the lilies of the field, how they grow; they neither toil nor spin; 29. yet I tell you, even Solomon in all his glory was not arrayed like one of these. 30. But if God so clothes the grass of the field, which today is alive and tomorrow is thrown into the oven, will he not much more clothe you, O men of little faith? 31. Therefore do not be anxious, saying, 'What shall we eat?' or 'What shall we drink?' or 'What shall we wear?' 32. For the Gentiles seek all these things; and your heavenly Father knows that you need them all. 33. But seek first his kingdom and his righteousness, and all these things shall be yours as well.

34. Therefore do not be anxious about tomorrow, for tomorrow will be anxious for itself. Let the day's own trouble be sufficient for the day."

True Devotion

#79. To rid ourselves of selfishness, we must first become thoroughly aware, by the light of the Holy Spirit, of our tainted nature. Of ourselves we are unable to do anything conducive to our salvation. Our human weakness is evident in everything we do and we are habitually unreliable. We do not deserve any grace from God.

Our tendency to sin is always present. The sin of Adam has almost entirely spoiled and soured us, filling us with pride and corrupting every one of us, just as leaven sours, swells and corrupts the dough in which it is placed. The actual sins we have committed, whether mortal or venial, even though forgiven, have intensified our base desires, our weakness, our inconstancy and our evil tendencies, and have left a sediment of evil in our soul.

Our bodies are so corrupt that they are referred to by the Holy Spirit (Rom. 6:6) as bodies of sin, as conceived and nourished in sin, and capable of any kind of sin. They are subject to a thousand ills, deteriorating from day to day and harboring only disease, vermin and corruption.

Our soul, being united to our body, has become so carnal that it has been called flesh. "All flesh had corrupted its way." (Gen. 6:12) Pride and blindness of spirit, hardness of heart, weakness and inconstancy of soul, evil inclinations, rebellious passions, ailments of body, - these are all we can call our own. By nature we are prouder than peacocks, we cling to the earth more than toads, we are baser than goats, more envious than serpents, greedier than pigs, fiercer than tigers, lazier than tortoises, weaker than reeds, and more changeable than weather-cocks. We have in us nothing but sin, and deserve only the wrath of God and eternity of hell. (Eph. 2:3)

#80. Is it any wonder then that our Lord laid down that anyone who aspires to be his follower must deny himself and hate his very life? He makes it clear that anyone who loves his life shall lose it and anyone who hates his life shall save it. Now, our Lord, who is infinite Wisdom, and does not give commandments without a reason, bids us hate ourselves only because we richly deserve to be hated. Nothing is more worthy of love than God and nothing is more deserving of hatred than self.

"Those who have great devotion to Mary not only will be saved but also will, through her intercession, become great Saints."
St. Vincent Palotti

FIFTEENTH DAY

Daily Prayers: *Litany of the Holy Ghost, Ave Maris Stella* and the *Holy Rosary.*

Daily Readings: Gospel of St. Matthew 7:1-29 and True Devotion #'s 81-82.

Church Teaching For Further Reading: Catechism of the Catholic Church #'s 2609, 1970, 1696, 678, 682, 2003, 585.

Gospel of St. Matthew 7:1-29 *Judge not, that you be not judged. 2. For with the judgment you pronounce you will be judged, and the measure you give will be the measure you get. 3. Why do you see the speck that is in your brother's eye, but do not notice the log that is in your own eye? 4. Or how can you say to your brother, 'Let me take the speck out of your eye,' when there is the log in your own eye? 5. You hypocrite, first take the log out of your own eye, and then you will see clearly to take the speck out of your brother's eye.*

6. Do not give dogs what is holy; and do not throw your pearls before swine, lest they trample them under foot and turn to attack you.

7. Ask, and it will be given you; seek, and you will find; knock, and it will be opened to you. 8. For every one who asks receives, and he who seeks finds, and to him who knocks it will be opened. 9. Or what man of you, if his son asks him for bread, will give him a stone? 10. Or if he asks for a fish, will give him a serpent? 11. If you then, who are evil, know how to give good gifts to your children, how much more will your Father who is in heaven give good things to those who ask him!

12. So whatever you wish that men would do to you, do so to them; for this is the law and the prophets.

13. Enter by the narrow gate; for the gate is wide and the way is easy, that leads to destruction, and those who enter by it are many. 14. For the gate is narrow and the way is hard, that leads to life, and those who find it are few.

15. Beware of false prophets, who come to you in sheep's clothing but inwardly are ravenous wolves. 16. You will know them by their fruits. Are grapes gathered from thorns, or figs from thistles? 17. So, every sound tree bears good fruit, but the bad tree bears evil fruit. 18. A sound tree cannot bear evil fruit, nor can a bad tree bear good fruit. 19. Every tree that does not bear good fruit is cut down and thrown into the fire. 20. Thus you will know them by their fruits.

21. Not every one who says to me, 'Lord, Lord,' shall enter the kingdom of heaven, but he who does the will of my Father who is in heaven. 22. On that day many will say to me, 'Lord, Lord, did we not prophesy in your name, and cast out demons in your name, and do mighty works in your name?' 23. And then will I declare to them, 'I never knew you; depart from me, you evildoers.'

24. Every one then who hears these words of mine and does them will be like a wise man who built his house upon the rock; 25. and the rain fell, and the floods came, and the winds blew and beat upon that house, but it did not fall, because it had been founded on the rock. 26. And every one who hears these words of mine and does not do them will be like a foolish man who built his house upon the sand; 27. and the rain fell, and the floods came, and the winds blew and beat against that house, and it fell; and great was the fall of it."

28. And when Jesus finished these sayings, the crowds were astonished at his teaching, 29. for he taught them as one who had authority, and not as their scribes.

True Devotion

#81. Secondly, in order to empty ourselves of self, we must die daily to ourselves. This involves our renouncing what the powers of the soul and the senses of the body incline us to do. We must see as if we did not see, hear as if we did not hear and use the things of this world as if we did not use them. This is what St. Paul calls "dying daily". Unless the grain of wheat falls to the ground and dies, it remains only a single grain and does not bear any good fruit. If we do not die to self and if our holiest devotions do not lead us to this necessary and fruitful death, we shall not bear fruit of any worth and our devotions will cease to be profitable. All our good works will be tainted by self-love and self-will so that our greatest sacrifices and our best actions will be unacceptable to God. Consequently when we come to die we shall find ourselves devoid of virtue and merit and discover that we do not possess even one spark of that pure love which God shares with only those who have died to themselves and whose life is hidden with Jesus Christ in him.

#82. Thirdly, we must choose among all the devotions to the Blessed Virgin the one which will lead us most surely to this dying to self. That devotion will be the best and most sanctifying for us. For

we must not believe that all that glitters is gold, all that is sweet is honey, or all that is easy to do and is done by the majority of people is the most sanctifying. Just as in nature there are secrets enabling us to do certain natural things quickly, easily and at little cost, so in the spiritual life there are secrets which enable us to perform supernatural works rapidly, smoothly and with facility. Such works are, for example, emptying ourselves of self-love, filling ourselves with God, and attaining perfection.

The devotion that I purpose to explain is one of these secrets of grace, for it is unknown to most Christians. Only a few devout people know of it and it is practiced and appreciated by fewer still. To begin the explanation of this devotion here is a fourth truth which is a consequence of the third.

"I heartily recommend True Devotion to the Blessed Virgin, so admirably written by Blessed De Montfort, and to all who read it I grant the Apostolic Benediction."
Pope St. Pius X

SIXTEENTH DAY

Daily Prayers: Litany of the Holy Ghost, Ave Maris Stella and the Holy Rosary.

Daily Readings: Gospel of St. Matthew 10:26-39; 12:33-37; 18:1-4; 19:13-15 and True Devotion #'s 83-84.

Church Teaching For Further Reading: Catechism of the Catholic Church #'s 1506, 2785, 1618-20, 1646, 1652.

Gospel of St. Matthew 10:26-39 *"So have no fear of them; for nothing is covered that will not be revealed, or hidden that will not be known. 27. What I tell you in the dark, utter in the light; and what you hear whispered, proclaim upon the housetops. 28. And do not fear those who kill the body but cannot kill the soul; rather fear him who can destroy both soul and body in hell. 29. Are not two sparrows sold for a penny? And not one of them will fall to the ground without your Father's will. 30. But even the hairs of your head are all numbered. 31. Fear not, therefore; you are of more value than many sparrows. 32. So every one who acknowledges me before men, I also will acknowledge before my Father who is in heaven; 33. but whoever denies me before men, I also will deny before my Father who is in heaven.*

34. Do not think that I have come to bring peace on earth; I have not come to bring peace, but a sword. 35. For I have come to set a man against his father, and a daughter against her mother, and a daughter-in-law against her mother-in-law; 36. and a man's foes will be those of his own household. 37. He who loves father or mother more than me is not worthy of me; and he who loves son or daughter more than me is not worthy of me; 38. and he who does not take his cross and follow me is not worthy of me. 39. He who finds his life will lose it, and he who loses his life for my sake will find it."

Gospel of St. Matthew 12:33-37 *"Either make the tree good, and its fruit good; or make the tree bad, and its fruit bad; for the tree is known by its fruit. 34. You brood of vipers! How can you speak good, when you are evil? For out of the abundance of the heart the mouth speaks. 35. The good man out of his good treasure brings forth good, and the evil man out of his evil treasure brings forth evil. 36. I tell you, on the day of judgment men will render account for every careless word they utter; 37. for by your words you will be justified, and by your words you will be condemned."*

Gospel of St. Matthew 18:1-4 At that time the disciples came to Jesus, saying, "Who is the greatest in the kingdom of heaven?" 2. And calling to him a child, he put him in the midst of them, 3. and said, *"Truly, I say to you, unless you turn and become like children, you will never enter the kingdom of heaven. 4. Whoever humbles himself like this child, he is the greatest in the kingdom of heaven."*

Gospel of St. Matthew 19:13-15 13. Then children were brought to him that he might lay his hands on them and pray. The disciples rebuked the people; 14. but Jesus said, *"Let the children come to me, and do not hinder them; for to such belongs the kingdom of heaven."* 15. And he laid hands on them and went away.

True Devotion

Fourth Principle: It is more humble to have an intermediary with Christ

#83. It is more perfect because it supposes greater humility to approach God through a mediator rather than directly by ourselves. Our human nature, as I have just shown, is so spoilt that if we rely on our own work, effort and preparedness to reach and please him, it is certain that our good works will be tainted and carry little weight with him. They will not induce him to unite himself to us or answer our prayers. God has his reasons for giving us mediators with him. He saw our unworthiness and helplessness and had pity on us. To give us access to his mercies he provided us with powerful advocates, so that to neglect these mediators and to approach his infinite holiness directly and without help from any one of them, is to be lacking humility and respect towards God who is so great and so holy. It would mean that we have less esteem for the King of kings than for an earthly king or ruler, for we would not dare approach an earthly king without a friend to speak for us.

#84. Our Lord is our Advocate and our Mediator of redemption with God the Father. It is through him that we must pray with the whole Church, triumphant and militant. It is through him that we have access to God the Father. We should never appear before God, our Father, unless we are supported by the merits of his Son, and, so to speak, clothed in them, as young Jacob was clothed in

the skin of the young goats when he appeared before his father Isaac to receive his blessing.

"Anything we may say in praise of Mary is little in comparison with what she deserves,
because of her dignity as Mother of God."
St. Augustine of Hippo

SEVENTEENTH DAY

Daily Prayers: *Litany of the Holy Ghost, Ave Maris Stella* and the *Holy Rosary.*

Daily Readings: Gospel of St. Luke 7:36-50; 9:23-27 and True Devotion #'s 85-86.

Church Teaching For Further Reading: Catechism of the Catholic Church #'s 546, 2712, 1435.

Gospel of St. Luke 7: 36-50   36. One of the Pharisees asked him to eat with him, and he went into the Pharisee's house, and sat at table. 37. And behold, a woman of the city, who was a sinner, when she learned that he was sitting at table in the Pharisee's house, brought an alabaster flask of ointment,   38. and standing behind him at his feet, weeping, she began to wet his feet with her tears, and wiped them with the hair of her head, and kissed his feet, and anointed them with the ointment.   39. Now when the Pharisee who had invited him saw it, he said to himself, "If this man were a prophet, he would have known who and what sort of woman this is who is touching him, for she is a sinner."   40. And Jesus answering said to him, *"Simon, I have something to say to you."* And he answered, "What is it, Teacher?"   41. *A certain creditor had two debtors; one owed five hundred denarii, and the other fifty.   42. When they could not pay, he forgave them both.   Now which of them will love him more?"*   43. Simon answered, "The one, I suppose, to whom he forgave more." And he said to him, *"You have judged rightly."*   44. Then turning toward the woman he said to Simon, *"Do you see this woman? I* *entered your house, you gave me no water for my feet, but she has wet my feet with her tears and wiped them with her hair. 45. You gave me no kiss, but from the time I came in she has not ceased to kiss my feet. 46. You did not anoint my head with oil, but she has anointed my feet with ointment. 47. Therefore I tell you, her sins, which are many, are forgiven, for she loved much; but he who is forgiven little, loves little."* 48. And he said to her, *"Your sins are forgiven."* 49. Then those who were at table with him began to say among themselves, "Who is this, who even forgives sins?" 50. And he said to the woman, *"Your faith has saved you; go in peace."*

Gospel of St. Luke 9:23-27 23. And he said to all, *"If any man would come after me, let him deny himself and take up his cross daily and follow me. 24. For whoever would save his life will lose it; and whoever loses his life for my sake, he will save it. 25. For what does it profit a man if he gains the whole world and loses or forfeits himself? 26. For whoever is ashamed of me and of my words, of him will the Son of man be ashamed when he comes in his glory and the glory of the Father and of the Holy angels. 27. But I tell you truly, there are some standing here who will not taste death before they see the kingdom of God."*

True Devotion

#85. But have we no need at all of a mediator with the Mediator himself? Are we pure enough to be united directly to Christ without any help? Is Jesus not God, equal in every way to the Father? Therefore is he not the Holy of Holies, having a right to the same

respect as his Father? If in his infinite love he became our security and our Mediator with his Father, whom he wished to appease in order to redeem us from our debts, should we on that account show him less respect and have less regard for the majesty and holiness of his person?

Let us not be afraid to say with St. Bernard that we need a mediator with Mediator himself and the divinely-honored Mary is the one most able to fulfill this office of love. Through her, Jesus came to us; through her, we should go to him. If we are afraid of going directly to Jesus, who is God, because of his infinite greatness, or our lowliness, or our sins, let us implore without fear the help and intercession of Mary, our Mother. She is kind, she is tender, and there is nothing harsh or forbidding about her, nothing too sublime or too brilliant. When we see her, we see but our own human nature. She is not the sun, dazzling our weak sight by the brightness of its rays. Rather, she is fair and gentle as the moon, which receives its light from the sun and softens it and adapts it to our limited perception.

She is so full of love that no one who asks for her intercession is rejected, no matter how sinful he may be. The saints say that it never has been known since the world began that anyone had recourse to our blessed Lady, with trust and perseverance, and was rejected. Her power is so great that her prayers are never refused. She has but to appear in prayer before her Son and he at once welcomes her and grants her requests. He is always lovingly conquered by the prayers of the dear Mother who bore him and nourished him.

#86. All this is taken from St. Bernard and St. Bonaventure. According to them, we have three steps to take in order to reach God. The first, nearest to us and most suited to our capacity is Mary; the second is Jesus Christ; the third is God the Father. To go to Jesus, we should go to Mary, our mediatrix of intercession. To go to God the Father, we must go to Jesus, our Mediator of Redemption. This order is perfectly observed in the devotion I shall speak about further on.

Mary is called "the Gate of Heaven because no one can enter that blessed Kingdom without passing through her."
St. Bonaventure

EIGHTEENTH DAY

Daily Prayers: Litany of the Holy Ghost, Ave Maris Stella and the Holy Rosary.

Daily Readings: Gospel of St. Luke 10:25-37; 12:13-21; 13:22-30 and True Devotion #'s 120-121.

Church Teaching For Further Reading: Catechism of the Catholic Church #'s 1825, 2447.

Gospel of St. Luke 10 25-37 25. And behold, a lawyer stood up to put him to the test, saying, "Teacher, what shall I do to inherit eternal life?" 26. He said to him, *"What is written in the law? How do you read?"* 27. And he answered, "You shall love the Lord your God with all your heart, and with all your soul, and with all your strength, and with all your mind; and your neighbor as yourself." 28. And he said to him, *"You have answered right; do this, and you will live."*

29. But he, desiring to justify himself, said to Jesus, "And who is my neighbor?" 30. Jesus replied, *"A man was going down from Jerusalem to Jericho, and he fell among robbers, who stripped him and beat him half dead. 31. Now by chance a priest was going down that road; and when he saw him he passed by on the other side. 32. So likewise a Levite, when he came to the place and saw him, passed by on the other side. 33. But a Samaritan, as he journeyed, came to where he was; and when he saw him, he had compassion, 34. and went to him and bound up his wounds, pouring on oil and wine; then he set him on his own beast and brought him to an inn, and took care of him. 35. And the next day he took out two denarii*

and gave them to the innkeeper, saying, 'Take care of him; and whatever more you spend, I will repay you when I come back. 36. Which of these three, do you think, proved neighbor to the man who fell among robbers?" 37. He said, "The one who showed mercy on him." And Jesus said to him, *"Go and do likewise."*

Gospel of St. Luke 12:13-21 13. One of the multitude said to him, "Teacher, bid my brother divide the inheritance with me." 14. But he said to him, "Man, who made me a judge or divider over you?" 15. And he said to them, **"***Take heed, and beware of all covetousness; for a man's life does not consist in the abundance of his possessions."* 16. And he told them a parable, saying, *"The land of a rich man brought forth plentifully; 17. and he thought to himself, 'What shall I do, for I have nowhere to store my crops?' 18. And he said, 'I will do this; I will pull down my barns, and build larger ones; and there I will store all my grain and my goods. 19. And I will say to my soul, Soul, you have ample goods laid up for many years; take your ease, eat, drink be merry.' 20. But God said to him, 'Fool! This night your soul is required of you; and the things you have prepared, whose will they be?' 21. So is he who lays up treasure for himself, and is not rich toward God."*

Gospel of St. Luke 13:22-30 22. He went on his way through towns and villages, teaching, and journeying toward Jerusalem. 23. And some one said to him, "Lord, will those who are saved be few?" And he said to them, *24. Strive to enter by the narrow door; for many, I tell you, will seek to enter and will not be able. 25. When* *once the householder has risen up and shut the door, you will begin to stand outside and to knock at the door, saying, 'Lord, open to us.' He will answer you, 'I do not know where you come from.' 26. Then you will begin to say, 'We ate and drank in your presence, and you taught in our streets.' 27. But he will say, 'I tell you, I do not know where you come from; depart from me, all you workers of iniquity!' 28. There you will weep and gnash your teeth, when you see Abraham and Isaac and Jacob and all the prophets in the kingdom of God and you yourselves thrust out. 29 And men will come from east and west, and from north and south, and sit at table in the kingdom of God. 30. And behold some are last who will be first, and some are first who will be last."*

True Devotion

THE PERFECT CONSECRATION TO JESUS CHRIST

1. A complete consecration to Mary

#120. As all perfection consists in our being conformed, united and consecrated to Jesus it naturally follows that the most perfect of all devotions is that which conforms, unites, and consecrates us most completely to Jesus. Now of all God's creatures Mary is the most conformed to Jesus. It therefore follows that, of all devotions, devotion to her makes for the most effective consecration and conformity to him. The more one is consecrated to Mary, the more one is consecrated to Jesus.

That is why perfect consecration to Jesus is but a perfect and complete consecration of oneself to the Blessed Virgin, which is the devotion I teach; or in other words, it is perfect renewal of the vows and promises of holy baptism.

#121. This devotion consists in giving oneself entirely to Mary in order to belong entirely to Jesus through her. It requires us to give:

1) Our body with its senses and members;

2) Our soul with its faculties;

3) Our present material possessions and all we shall acquire in the future;

4) Our interior and spiritual possessions, that is, our merits, virtues and good actions of the past, the present and the future.

In other words, we give her all that we posses both in our natural life and in our spiritual life, as well as everything we shall acquire in the future in the order of nature, of grace, and of glory in heaven. This we do without any reservation, not even of a penny, a hair, or the smallest good deed. And we give for all eternity without claiming or expecting, in return for our offering and our service, any other reward than the honor of belonging to our Lord through Mary and in Mary, even though our Mother were not - as in fact she always is - the most generous and appreciative of all God's creatures.

"From the moment when this Virgin Mother conceived the Divine Word in her womb, she acquired a special jurisdiction, so to say, over all the graces of the Holy Spirit."
St. Bernardine of Siena

NINETEENTH DAY

Daily Prayers: Litany of the Holy Ghost, Ave Maris Stella and the Holy Rosary.

Daily Readings: Gospel of St. Luke 15:1-32; 18:9-14,18-30 and True Devotion #'s 122-125.

Church Teaching For Further Reading: Catechism of the Catholic Church #'s 545, 1443, 1439, 2839, 588, 2559, 2839.

Gospel of St. Luke 15:1-32 Now the tax collectors and sinners were all drawing near to hear him. 2. And the Pharisees and the scribes murmured, saying, "This man receives sinners and eats with them."

3. So he told them this parable: *4. "What man of you, having a hundred sheep, if he has lost one of them, does not leave the ninety-nine in the wilderness, and go after the one which is lost, until he finds it? 5. And when he has found it, he lays it on his shoulders, rejoicing. 6. And when he comes home, he calls together his friends and his neighbors, saying to them, 'Rejoice with me, for I have found my sheep which was lost.' 7. Just so, I tell you, there will be more joy in heaven over one sinner who repents than over ninety-nine righteous persons who need no repentance.*

8. Or what woman, having ten silver coins, if she loses one coin, does not light a lamp and sweep the house and seek diligently until she finds it? 9. And when she has found it, she calls together her friends and neighbors, saying, 'Rejoice with me, for I have found the coin which I had lost.' 10. Just so, I tell you, there is joy before the angels of God over one sinner who repents."

11. And he said, "There was a man who had two sons; 12. and the younger of them said to his father, 'Father, give me the share of property that falls to me.' And he divided his living between them. 13 Not many days later the younger son gathered all he had and took his journey into a far country, and there he squandered his property in loose living. 14. And when he has spent everything, a great famine arose in that country, and he began to be in want. 15. So he went and joined himself to one of the citizens of that country, who sent him into his fields to feed swine. 16. And he would gladly have fed on the pods that the swine ate; and no one gave him anything. 17. But when he came to himself he said, 'How many of my father's hired servants have bread enough and to spare, but I perish here with hunger! 18. I will arise and go to my father, and I will say to him, "Father, I have sinned against heaven and before you; 19. I am no longer worthy to be called your son; treat me as one of your hired servants."' 20. And he arose and come to his father. But while he was yet at a distance, his father saw him and had compassion, and ran and embraced him and kissed him. 21. And the son said to him, 'Father, I have sinned against heaven and before you; I am no longer worthy to be called your son.' 22. But the father said to his servants, 'Bring quickly the best robe, and put it on him; and put a ring on his hand, and shoes on his feet; 23. and bring the fatted calf and kill it, and let us eat and make merry; 24. for this my son was dead, and is alive again; he was lost, and is found.' And they began to make merry.

25. Now his elder son was in the field; and as he came and drew near to the house, he heard music and dancing. 26. And he called one of the servants and asked what this meant. 27. And he said to him, 'Your brother has come, and your father has killed the fatted calf, because he has received him safe and sound.' 28. But he was angry and refused to go in. His father come out and entreated him, 29. but he answered his father, 'Lo, these many years I have served you, and I never disobeyed your command; yet you never gave me a kid, that I might make merry with my friends. 30. But when this son of yours came, who has devoured your living with harlots, you killed for him the fatted calf!' 31. And he said to him, 'Son, you are always with me, and all that is mine is yours. 32. It was fitting to make merry and be glad, for this your brother was dead, and is alive; he was lost, and is found.'"

Gospel of St. Luke 18:9-14 He also told this parable to some who trusted in themselves that they were righteous and despised others: *10. "Two men went up into the temple to pray, on a Pharisee and the other a tax collector. 11. The Pharisee stood and prayed thus with himself, 'God, I thank thee that I am not like other men, extortioners, unjust, adulterers, or even like this tax collector. 12. I fast twice a week, I give tithes of all that I get.' 13. But the tax collector, standing far off, would not even lift up his eyes to heaven, but beat his breast, saying 'God, be merciful to me a sinner!' 14. I tell you, this man went down to his house justified rather than the other; for every one who exalts himself will be humbled, but he who humbles himself will be exalted."*

Gospel of St. Luke 18:18-30   And a ruler asked him, "Good Teacher, what shall I do to inherit eternal life?" 19. And Jesus said to him, *"Why do you call me good? No one is good but God alone. You know the commandments: 'Do not commit adultery, Do not kill, do not steal, Do not bear false witness, Honor your father and mother.'"* 21. And he said, "All these I have observed from my youth." 22. And when Jesus heard it he said to him, *"One thing you still lack. Sell all that you have and distribute to the poor, and you will have treasure in heaven; and come, follow me."* 23. But when he heard this he became sad, for he was very rich. 24. Jesus looking at him said, *"How hard it is for those who have riches to enter the kingdom of God! 25. For it is easier for a camel to go through the eye of a needle than for a rich man to enter the kingdom of God."* 26. Those who heard it said, "Then who can be saved?" 27. But he said, *"What is impossible with men is possible with God."* 28. And Peter said, "Lo, we have left our homes and followed you." 29. And he said to them, *"Truly, I say to you, there is no man who has left house or wife or brothers or parents or children, for the sake of the kingdom of God, 30. who will not receive manifold more in this time, and in the age to come eternal life."*

True Devotion

#122.   Note here that two things must be considered regarding our good works, namely, satisfaction and merit or, in other words, their satisfactory or prayer value and their meritorious value. The satisfactory or prayer value of good work is the good action in so

far as it makes condign atonement for the punishment due to sin or obtains some new grace. The meritorious value or merit is the good action in so far as it merits grace and eternal glory. Now by this consecration of ourselves to the Blessed Virgin we give her all satisfactory and prayer value as well as the meritorious value of our good works, in other words, all the satisfactions and the merits. We give her our merits, graces and virtues, not that she might give them to others, for they are, strictly speaking, not transferable, because Jesus alone, in making himself our surety with his Father, had the power to impart his merits to us. But we give them to her that she may keep, increase and embellish them for us, as we shall explain later, and we give her our acts of atonement that she may apply them where she pleases for God's greater glory.

#123. It follows then: 1) that by this devotion we give to Jesus all we can possibly give him, and in the most perfect manner, that is, through Mary's hands. Indeed we give him far more than we do by other devotions which require us to give only part of our time some of our good works or acts of atonement and penances. In this devotion everything is given and consecrated, even the rights to dispose freely of one's spiritual goods and the satisfactions earned by daily good works. This is not done even in religious orders. Members of religious orders give God their earthly goods by the vow of poverty, the goods of the body by the vow of chastity, their free will by the vow of obedience, and sometimes their freedom of movement by the vow of enclosure. But they do not despoil themselves of what a Christian considers most precious and most dear - his merits and satisfactions.

#124. 2) It follows then that anyone who in this way consecrates and sacrifices himself voluntary to Jesus through Mary may no longer dispose of the value of any of his good actions. All his sufferings, all his thoughts, words, and deeds belong to Mary. She can then dispose of them in accordance with the will of her Son and for his greater glory. This dependence, however, is without detriment to the duties of a person's present and future state of life. One such duty, for example, would be that of a priest who, by virtue of his office or otherwise, must apply the satisfactory or prayer value of the Mass to a particular person. For this consecration can only be made in accordance with the order established by God and in keeping with the duties of one's state of life

#125. 3) It follows that we consecrate ourselves at one and the same time to Mary and to Jesus. We give ourselves to Mary because Jesus chose her as the perfect means to unite himself to us and unite us to him. We give ourselves to Jesus because he is our last end. Since he is our Redeemer and our God we are indebted to him for all that we are.

"Let all hearts give themselves to Mary so that she may fill them with her heart and the Heart of Jesus!"
St. John Eudes

Third Period Theme
Knowledge of the Blessed Virgin Mary

Next Seven Days

During the second week you should apply yourself, in all your prayers and works each day, to know the Blessed Virgin. You should ask this knowledge of the Holy Ghost. You must unite yourself to Jesus through Mary-this is the characteristic of devotion; therefore, Saint Louis De Montfort asks that the second week be employed in acquiring a knowledge of the Blessed Virgin.

Mary is your sovereign and your mediatrix, you Mother and your Mistress. Endeavor then to know the effects of the royalty, of this mediation, and of this maternity, as well as the grandeurs and prerogatives which are the foundation or consequences thereof. Our Mother is also a perfect mold wherein you are to be molded in order to make her intentions and dispositions yours. This you cannot achieve without studying the interior life of Mary; namely, her virtues, her sentiments, her actions, her participation in the mysteries of Christ and her union with Him.

Daily Prayers: *Litany to the Blessed Virgin, Ave Maris Stella,* Saint Louis De Montfort's *Prayer to Mary* and the *Holy Rosary.*

Spiritual Exercises during the Second Week are: Acts of Love, pious affections for the Blessed Virgin, imitation of her virtues, especially continual mental prayer, her mortification in all things, her divine purity, her ardent charity, her heroic patience, her angelic sweetness and her divine wisdom; "these being," as Saint Louis De Montfort says, "the ten principal virtues of the Blessed Virgin."

Mary's Immaculate Conception

The next seven days, Knowledge of Mary, will be dedicated to Mary's Immaculate Conception. This *de fide* dogma was proclaimed in 1854 by Pope Pius IX in *Ineffabilis Deus*. It states, "The most Blessed Virgin Mary was, from the first moment of her conception, by a singular grace and privilege of almighty God and by virtue of the merits of Jesus Christ, Savior of the human race, preserved immune from all stain of original sin."

A common misunderstanding for some reason in our day, is that the term Immaculate Conception refers to Jesus' birth, but as we have just read in the proclamation that the Immaculate Conception refers to the Blessed Virgin Mary's conception. There was never any sin, original, actual sin or even concupiscence, that ever touched the soul and body of the Blessed Mother. She was "preserved" immune and not "transformed" as some may understand it today, by the foreseen merits of Jesus' death on the cross. In addition, the definition states that this was a "singular grace", given only to the Blessed Mother. Therefore, no one has or ever will be conceived immaculately. To put it simply, the Blessed Mother was conceived immaculately because she was to give birth to Jesus, our sinless, Immaculate Victim, given to us for our salvation. In addition, if the Blessed Mother had sinned even for an instant, she would have been an enemy of God which would have rendered her unworthy to be the Mother of God and to participate with her Son in our redemption as prophesied in Genesis 3:15.

The support of this dogma in Sacred Scripture is found in Genesis 3:15, Luke 1:28 and in the Catechism of the Catholic Church #'s 490-493.

TWENTIETH DAY

Daily Prayers: *Litany of the Blessed Virgin, Ave Maris Stella,* Saint De Montfort's *Prayer to Mary* and the *Holy Rosary.*

Daily Readings: Gospel of St. Luke 1:26-38 and True Devotion #'s 14-21.

Church Teaching For Further Reading: Catechism of the Catholic Church #'s 490-93, 430, 437, 709-10, 497, 723.

Gospel of St. Luke 1:26-38 In the sixth month the angel Gabriel was sent from God to a city of Galilee named Nazareth, 27. to a virgin betrothed to a man whose name was Joseph, of the house of David; and the virgin's name was Mary. 28. And he came to her and said, "Hail, full of grace, the Lord is with you!" 29. But she was greatly troubled at the saying, and considered in her mind what sort of greeting this might be. 30. And the angel said to her, "Do not be afraid, Mary, for you have found favor with God. 31. And behold, you will conceive in your womb and bear a son, and you shall call his name Jesus.

32. He will be great, and will be called the Son of the Most High; and the Lord God will give to him the throne of his father David, 33. and he will reign over the house of Jacob for ever; and of his kingdom there will be no end." 34. And Mary said to the angel, "How can this be, since I have no husband?" 35. And the angel said to her, "The Holy Spirit will come upon you, and the power of the Most High will overshadow you; therefore the child to be born will

be called holy, the Son of God. 36. And behold, your kinswoman Elizabeth in her old age has also conceived a son; and this is the sixth month with her who was called barren. 37. For with God nothing will be impossible." 38. And Mary said, "Behold, I am the handmaid of the Lord; let it be to me according to your word." And the angel departed from her.

True Devotion

NECESSITY OF DEVOTION TO OUR LADY

2. *Mary's part in the Incarnation*

#14. With the whole Church I acknowledge that Mary, being a mere creature fashioned by the hands of God is, compared to his infinite majesty, less than an atom, or rather is simply nothing, since he alone can say, "I am he who is". (Exod. 3:14) Consequently, this great Lord, who is ever independent and self-sufficient, never had and does not now have any absolute need of the Blessed Virgin for the accomplishment of his will and the manifestation of his glory. To do all things he has only to will them.

#15. However, I declare that, considering things as they are, because God has decided to begin and accomplish his greatest works through the Blessed Virgin ever since he created her, we can safely believe that he will not change his plan in the time to come, for he is God and therefore does not change in his thoughts or his way of acting. (Heb. 1:12; Ps. 101:28)

#16. God the Father gave his only Son to the world only through Mary. Whatever desires the patriarchs may have cherished, whatever entreaties the prophets and saints of the Old Law may have made for 4,000 years to obtain that treasure, it was Mary alone who merited it and found grace before God by the power of her prayers and the perfection of her virtues, "The world being unworthy," said St. Augustine, "to receive the Son of God directly from the hands of the Father, he gave his Son to Mary for the world to receive him from her".

The Son of God became man for our salvation but only in Mary and through Mary.

God the Holy Spirit formed Jesus Christ in Mary but only after having asked her consent through one of the chief ministers of his court.

#17. God the Father imparted to Mary his fruitfulness as far as a mere creature was capable of receiving it, to enable her to bring forth his Son and all the members of his mystical body.

#18. God the Son came down into her virginal womb as a new Adam into his earthly paradise, to take his delight there and produce hidden wonders of grace.

God-made-man found freedom in imprisoning himself in her womb. He displayed power in allowing himself to be borne by this young maiden. He found his glory and that of his Father in hiding his splendors from all creatures here below and revealing them only to Mary. He glorified his independence and his majesty in depending upon this lovable virgin in his conception, his birth, his presentation in the temple, and in the thirty years of his hidden life. Even at his death she had to be present so that he might be united with her in one sacrifice and be immolated with her consent to the eternal Father, just as formerly Isaac was offered in sacrifice by Abraham when he accepted the will of God. It was Mary who nursed him, fed him, cared for him, reared him, and sacrificed him for us.

The Holy Spirit could not leave such wonderful and inconceivable dependence of God unmentioned in the Gospel, though he concealed almost all the wonderful things that Wisdom Incarnate did during his hidden life in order to bring home to us its infinite value and glory. Jesus gave more glory to God his Father by submitting to his Mother for thirty years than he would have given him had he converted the whole world by working the greatest miracles. How highly then do we glorify God when to please him we submit ourselves to Mary, taking Jesus as our sole model!

#19. If we examine closely the remainder of the life of Jesus Christ, we see that he chose to begin his miracles through Mary. It was by her word that he sanctified St. John the Baptist in the womb of his mother, St. Elizabeth; no sooner had Mary spoken than John was sanctified. This was his first and greatest miracle of grace. At the wedding in Cana he changed water into wine at her humble prayer, and this was his first miracle in the order of nature. He began and continued them through her until the end of time.

#20. God the Holy Spirit, who does not produce any divine person, became fruitful through Mary whom he espoused. It was with her, in her and of her that he produced his masterpiece, God-made-man, and that he produces every day until the end of the world the members of the body of this adorable Head. For this reason the more

he finds Mary, his dear and inseparable spouse, in a soul the more powerful and effective he becomes in producing Jesus Christ in that soul and that soul in Jesus Christ.

#21. This does not mean that the Blessed Virgin confers on the Holy Spirit a fruitfulness which he does not already posses. Being God, he has the ability to produce just like the Father and the Son, although he does not use this power and so does not produce another divine person. But it does mean that the Holy Spirit chose to make use of our Blessed Lady, although he had no absolute need of her, in order to become actively fruitful in producing Jesus Christ and his members in her and by her. This is a mystery of grace unknown even to many of the most learned and spiritual of Christians.

"In order to understand more accurately Who the Immaculate is, it is absolutely necessary to admit one's total nothingness, to bring oneself to humble prayer in order to gain the grace of knowing Her, and to endeavor personally to experience Her goodness and power."

St. Maximilian Mary Kolbe

TWENTY-FIRST DAY

Daily Prayers: Litany of the Blessed Virgin, Ave Maris Stella, Prayer to Mary and the Holy Rosary.

Daily Day Readings: Gospel of St. Luke 1:39-45 and True Devotion #'s 135-143.

Church Teaching For Further Reading: Catechism of the Catholic Church #'s 148, 494, 2617, 64, 489, 449, 495.

Gospel of St. Luke 1:39-45 39. In those days Mary arose and went with haste in to the hill country, to a city of Judah, 40. and she entered the house of Zechariah and greeted Elizabeth. 41. And when Elizabeth heard the greeting of Mary, the babe leaped in her womb; and Elizabeth was filled with the Holy Spirit 42. and she exclaimed with a loud cry, "Blessed are you among women, and blessed is the fruit of your womb! 43. And why is this granted me, that the mother of my Lord should come to me? 44. For behold, when the voice of your greeting came to my ears, the babe in my womb leaped for joy. 45. And blessed is she who believed that there would be a fulfillment of what was spoken to her from the Lord."

46. And Mary said, "My soul magnifies the Lord, 47. and my spirit rejoices in God my Savior, 48. for he has regarded the low estate of his handmaiden. For behold, henceforth all generations will call me blessed; 49. for he who is mighty has done great things for me, and holy is his name. 50. And his mercy is on those who fear him from generation to generation. 51. He has shown strength with his arm, he has scattered the proud in the imagination of their hearts,

52. he has put down the mighty from their thrones, and exalted those of low degree; 53. he has filled the hungry with good things, and the rich he has sent empty away. 54. He has helped his servant Israel, in remembrance of his mercy, 55. as he spoke to our fathers, to Abraham and to his posterity for ever." 56. And Mary remained with her about three months, and returned to her home.

True Devotion

MOTIVES WHICH RECOMMEND THIS DEVOTION

1. By it we give ourselves completely to God

#135. This first motive shows us the excellence of the consecration of ourselves to Jesus through Mary.

We can conceive of no higher calling than that of being in the service of God and we believe that the least of God's servants is richer, stronger and nobler than any earthly monarch who does not serve God. How rich and strong and noble then must the good and faithful servant be, who serves God as unreservedly and as completely as he possible can! Just such a person is the faithful and loving slave of Jesus and Mary. He has indeed surrendered himself entirely to the service of the King of kings through Mary, his Mother, keeping nothing for himself. All the gold of the world and the beauties of the heavens could not recompense him for what he has done.

#136. Other congregations, associations and confraternities set up in honor of our Lord and our Blessed Lady, which do so much good in the Church, do not require their members to give up absolutely everything. They simply prescribe for them the performance of certain acts and practices in fulfillment of their obligations. They leave them free to dispose of the rest of their actions as well as their time. But this devotion makes us give Jesus and Mary all our thoughts, words, actions, and sufferings and every moment of our lives without exception. Thus, whatever we do, whether we are awake or asleep, whether we eat or drink, whether we do important or unimportant work, it will always be true to say that everything is done for Jesus and Mary. Our offering always holds good, whether we think of it or not, unless we explicitly retract it. How consoling this is!

#137. Moreover, as I have said before, no other act of devotion enables us to rid ourselves so easily of the possessiveness which slips unnoticed even into our best actions. This is a remarkable grace which our dear Lord grants us in return for the heroic and selfless surrender to him through Mary of the entire value of our good works. If even in this life he gives a hundredfold reward to those who renounce all material, temporal and perishable things out of love for him, how generously will he reward those who give up even interior and spiritual goods for his sake!

#138. Jesus, our dearest friend, gave himself to us without reserve, body and soul, graces and merits. As St. Bernard says, "He won me over entirely by giving himself entirely to me." Does not simple justice as well as gratitude require that we give him all we

possibly can? He was generous with us first, so let us be generous to him in return and he will prove still more generous to us during life, at the hour of death, and throughout eternity. "He will be generous towards the generous."

2. It helps us to imitate Christ

#139. Our good Master stopped to enclose himself in the womb the Blessed Virgin, a captive and loving slave, and to make himself subject to her for thirty years. As I said earlier, the human mind is bewildered when it reflects seriously upon this conduct of Incarnate Wisdom. He did not choose to give himself in a direct manner to the human race though he could easily have done so. He chose to come through the Virgin Mary. Thus he did not come into the world independently of others in the flower of his manhood, but he came as a frail little child dependent on the care and attention of his Mother. Consumed with the desire to give glory of God, his Father, and save the human race, he saw no better or shorter way to do so than by submitting completely to Mary.

He did this not just for the first eight, ten or fifteen years of his life like other children, but for thirty years. He gave more glory to God, his Father, during all those years of submission and dependence then he would have given by spending them working miracles, preaching far and wide, and converting all mankind. Otherwise he would have done all these things.

What immeasurable glory then do we give to God when, following the example of Jesus, we submit to Mary! With such a convincing and well-known example before us, can we be so foolish as to believe that there is a better and shorter way of giving God glory than by submitting ourselves to Mary, as Jesus did?

#140. Let me remind you again of the dependence shown by the three divine Persons on our Blessed Lady. Theirs is the example which fully justifies our dependence on her. The Father gave and still gives his son only through her. He raises children for himself only through her. He dispenses his graces to us only through her. God the Son was prepared for mankind in general by her alone. Mary, in union with the Holy Spirit, still conceives him and brings him forth daily. It is through her alone that the Son distributes his merits and virtues. The Holy Spirit formed Jesus only through her, and he forms the members of the Mystical Body and dispenses his gifts and his favors through her.

With such a compelling example of the three divine Persons before us, we would be extremely perverse to ignore her and not consecrate ourselves to her. Indeed we would be blind if we did not see the need for Mary in approaching God and making our total offering to him.

#141. Here are a few passages from the Fathers of the Church which I have chosen to prove what I have just said:

"Mary has two sons, the one a God-man, the other, mere man. She is Mother of the first corporally and of the second spiritually" (St. Bonaventure and Origen).

This is the will of God who willed that we should have all things through Mary. If then, we possess any hope or grace or gift of salvation, let us acknowledge that it comes to us through her" (St. Bernard).

"All the gifts, graces, virtues of the Holy Spirit are distributed by the hands of Mary, to whom she wills, when she wills, as she wills, and in the measure she wills" (St. Bernardine).

"As you were not worthy that anything divine should be given to you, all graces were given to Mary so that you might receive through her all graces you would not otherwise receive" (St. Bernard).

#142. St. Bernard tells us that God, seeing that we are unworthy to receive his graces directly from him, gives them to Mary so that we might receive from her all that he decides to give us. His glory is achieved when he receives through Mary the gratitude, respect and love we owe him in return for his gifts to us. It is only right then that we should imitate his conduct, "in order", as St. Bernard again says, "that grace might return to its author by the same channel through which it came to us."

This is what we do by this devotion. We offer and consecrate all we are and all we possess to the Blessed Virgin in order that our Lord may receive through her as intermediary the glory and gratitude that we owe to him. We deem ourselves unworthy and unfit to approach his infinite majesty on our own, and so we avail ourselves of Mary's intercession.

#143. Moreover, this devotion is an expression of great humility, a virtue which God loves above all others. A person who exalts himself debases God, and a person who humbles himself exalts God. "God opposes the proud, but gives his graces to the

humble." (James 4:6) If you humble yourself, convinced that you are unworthy to appear before him, or even to approach him, he condescends to come down to you. He is pleased to be with you and exalts you in spite of yourself. But, on the other hand, if you venture to go towards God boldly without a mediator, he vanishes and is nowhere to be found. How dearly he loves the humble of heart! It is to such humility that this devotion leads us, for it teaches us never to go alone directly to our Lord, however gentle and merciful though he may be, but always to use Mary's power of intercession, whether we want to enter his presence, speak to him, be near him, offer him something, seek union with him or consecrate ourselves to him.

"When you say your Rosary, the angels rejoice,
the Blessed Trinity delights in it, my Son finds joy in it too,
and I myself am happier than you can possibly guess.
After the Holy Sacrifice of the Mass,
there is nothing in the Church that I love as much as the Rosary."

Our Lady to Blessed Alan de la Roche

TWENTY-SECOND DAY

Daily Prayers: Litany of the Blessed Virgin, Ave Maris Stella, Prayers to Mary and the Holy Rosary.

Daily Readings: Gospel of St. Luke 2:25-35 and True Devotion #'s 144-150.

Church Teaching For Further Reading: Catechism of the Catholic Church #'s 529, 587, 618.

Gospel of St. Luke 2:25-35 25. Now there was a man in Jerusalem, whose name was Simeon, and this man was righteous and devout, looking for the consolation of Israel, and the Holy Spirit was upon him. 26. And it had been revealed to him by the Holy Spirit that he should not see death before he had seen the Lord's Christ. 27. And inspired by the Spirit he came into the temple; and when the parents brought in the child Jesus, to do for him according to the custom of the law, 28. he took him up in his arms and blessed God and said, 29. "Lord, now lettest thou thy servant depart in peace, according to thy word; 30. for mine eyes have seen thy salvation 31. which thou hast prepared in the presence of all peoples, 32. a light for revelation to the Gentiles, and for glory to thy people Israel." 33. And his father and his mother marveled at what was said about him; 34. and Simeon blessed them and said to Mary his mother, "Behold, this child is set for the fall and rising of many in Israel, and for a sign that is spoken against 35. (and a sword will pierce through your own soul also), that thoughts out of many hearts may be revealed."

True Devotion

1. It obtains many blessings from our Lady

#144. The Blessed Virgin, mother of gentleness and mercy, never allows herself to be surpassed in love and generosity. When she sees someone giving himself entirely to her in order to honor and serve her, and depriving himself of what he prizes most in order to adorn her, she gives herself completely in a wondrous manner to him. She engulfs him in the ocean of her graces, adorns him with her merits, supports him with her power, enlightens him with her light, and fills him with her love. She shares her virtues with him - her humility, faith, purity, etc. She makes up for his failings and becomes his representative with Jesus. Just as one who is consecrated belongs entirely to Mary, so Mary belongs entirely to him. We can truthfully say of this perfect servant and child of Mary what St. John in his gospel says of himself, "He took her for his own."

#145. This produces in his soul, if he is persevering, a great distrust, contempt, and hatred of self, and a great confidence in Mary with complete self-abandonment to her. He no longer relies on his own dispositions, intentions, merits, virtues and good works, since he has sacrificed them completely to Jesus through his loving Mother. He has now only one treasury, where all his wealth is stored. That treasury is not within himself: it is Mary. That is why he can now go to our Lord without any servile or scrupulous fear and pray to him with great confidence. He can share the sentiments of the devout and learned Abbot Rupert, who, referring to the victory which Jacob won over the angel, (Gen. 32:25) addressed our Lady in these words, "O

Mary, my Queen, Immaculate Mother of the God-man, Jesus Christ, I desire to wrestle with this man, the Divine Word, armed with your merits and not my own."

How much stronger and more powerful are we in approaching our Lord when we are armed with the merits and prayers of the worthy Mother of God, who, as St. Augustine says, has conquered the Almighty by her love!

#146. Since by this devotion we give to our Lord, through the hands of his holy Mother, all our good works, she purifies them, making them beautiful and acceptable to her Son.

1). She purifies them of every taint of self-love and of that unconscious attachment to creatures which slips unnoticed into our best actions. Her hands have never been known to be idle or uncreative. They purify everything they touch. As soon as the Blessed Virgin receives our good works, she removes any blemish or imperfection she may find in them.

#147. 2) She enriches our good works by adorning them with her own merits and virtues. It is as if a poor peasant, wishing to win the friendship and favor of the king, were to go to the queen and give her an apple - his only possession - for her to offer it to the king. The queen, accepting the peasant's humble gift, puts it on a beautiful golden dish and presents it to the king on behalf of the peasant. The apple in itself would not be a gift worthy of a king, but presented by the queen in person on a dish of gold, it becomes fit for any king.

#148. 3) Mary presents our good works to Jesus. She does not keep anything we offer for herself, as if she were our last end, but unfailingly gives everything to Jesus. So by the very fact we give

anything to her, we are giving it to Jesus. Whenever we praise and glorify her, she immediately praises and glorifies Jesus. When anyone praises and blesses her, she sings today as she did on the day Elizabeth praised her, *"My soul glorifies the Lord."*

#149. At Mary's request, Jesus accepts the gift of our good works, no matter how poor and insignificant they may be for one who is the King of kings, the Holiest of the holy. When we present anything to Jesus by ourselves, relying on our own dispositions and efforts, he examines our gift and often rejects it because it is stained with self-love, imbued with selfish motives.

But when we present something to him by the pure, virginal hands of his beloved Mother, we take him by his weak side, in a manner of speaking. He does not consider so much the present itself as the person who offers it. Thus Mary, who is never slighted by her Son but is always well received, prevails upon him to accept with pleasure everything she offers him, regardless of its value. This is what St. Bernard strongly recommended to all those he was guiding along the pathway to perfection. *"When you want to offer something to God, to be welcomed by him be sure to offer it through the worthy Mother of God, if you do not wish to see it rejected."*

#150. Does not human nature itself, as we have seen, suggest this mode of procedure to the less important people of this world with regard to the great? Why should grace not inspire us to do likewise with regard to God? He is infinitely exalted above us. We are less than atoms in his sight. But we have an advocate so powerful that she is never refused anything. She is so resourceful that she knows every secret way to win the heart of God. She is so good and

106

kind that she never passes over anyone no matter how lowly and sinful.

Further on, I shall relate the story of Jacob and Rebecca which exemplifies the truths I have been setting before you.

"If you persevere in reciting the Rosary, this will be a most probable sign of your eternal salvation."
Blessed Alan de la Roche

TWENTY-THIRD DAY

Daily Prayers: Litany of the Blessed Virgin, Ave Maris Stella, Prayer to Mary and the Holy Rosary.

Daily Readings: Gospel of St. John 2:1-12 and True Devotion #'s 151-158.

Church Teaching For Further Reading: Catechism of the Catholic Church #'s 1613, 969, 494, 2618, 796, 1335.

Gospel of St. John 2:1-12 On the third day there was a marriage at Cana in Galilee, and the mother of Jesus was there; 2. Jesus also was invited to the marriage, with his disciples. 3. When the wine failed, the mother of Jesus said to him, "They have no wine." 4. And Jesus said to her, *"O woman, what have you to do with me? My hour has not yet come."* 5. His mother said to the servants, "Do whatever he tells you." 6. Now six stone jars were standing there, for the Jewish rites of purification, each holding twenty or thirty gallons. 7. Jesus said to them, *"Fill the jars with water."* And they filled them up to the brim. 8. He said to them, *"Now draw some out, and take it to the steward of the feast."* So they took it. 9. When the steward of the feast tasted the water now become wine, and did not know where it came from (though the servants who had drawn the water knew), the steward of the feast called the bridegroom 10. and said to him, "Every man serves the good wine first; and when men have drunk freely, then the poor wine; but you have kept the good wine until now." 11. This, the first of his signs, Jesus did at Cana in Galilee, and manifested his glory; and his disciples believed in him.

True Devotion

1. It is an excellent means of giving glory to God

#151. This devotion, when faithfully undertaken, is a perfect means of ensuring that the value of all our good works is being used for the greater glory of God. Scarcely anyone works for that noble end, in spite of the obligation to do so, either because men do not know where God's greatest glory is to be found or because they do not desire it. Now Mary, to whom we surrender the value and merit of our good actions, knows perfectly well where God's greatest glory lies and she works only to promote that glory.

The devout servant of our Lady, having entirely consecrated himself to her as we have described above, can boldly claim that the value of all his actions, words, and thoughts is used for the greatest glory of God, unless he has explicitly retracted his offering. For one who loves God with a pure and unselfish love and prizes God's glory and interests far above his own, could anything be more consoling?

5. It leads to union with our Lord

#152. This devotion is a smooth, short, perfect and sure way of attaining union with our Lord, in which Christian perfection consists.

1) *This devotion is a smooth way.* It is the path which Jesus Christ opened up in coming to us and in which there is no obstruction to prevent our reaching him. It is quite true that we can attain to divine union by other roads, but these involve many more crosses and exceptional setbacks and many difficulties that we cannot easily overcome. We would have to pass through spiritual darkness, engage in struggles for which we are not prepared, endure bitter agonies, scale precipitous mountains, tread upon painful thorns, and cross frightful deserts. But when we take the path of Mary, we walk smoothly and calmly.

It is true that on our way we have hard battles to fight and serious obstacles to overcome, but Mary, our Mother and Queen, stays close to her faithful servants. She is always at hand to brighten their darkness, clear away their doubts, strengthen them in their fears, sustain them in their combats and trials. Truly, in comparison with other ways, this virgin road to Jesus is a path of roses and sweet delights. There have been some saints, not very many, such as St. Ephrem, St. John Damascene, St. Bernard, St. Bernardine, St. Bonaventure and St. Francis de Sales, who have taken this smooth path to Jesus Christ, because the Holy Spirit, the faithful Spouse of Mary, made it known to them by a special grace. The other saints, who are the greater number, while having a devotion to Mary, either did not enter or did not go far along this path. That is why they had to undergo harder and more dangerous trials.

#153. Why is it then, a servant of Mary might ask, that devoted servants of this good Mother are called upon to suffer much more than those who serve her less generously? They are opposed, persecuted, slandered, and treated with intolerance. They may also have to walk in interior darkness and through spiritual deserts without being given from heaven a single drop of the dew of consolation. If this devotion to the Blessed Virgin makes the path to Jesus smoother, how can we explain why Mary's royal servants are so ill-treated?

#154. I reply that it is quite true that the most faithful servants of the Blessed Virgin, being her greatest favorites, receive from her the best graces and favors from heaven, which are crosses. But I maintain too that these servants of Mary bear their crosses with greater ease and gain more merit and glory. What could check another's progress a thousand times over, or possibly bring about his downfall, does not balk them at all, but even helps them on their way. For this good Mother, filled with the grace and unction of the Holy Spirit, dips all the crosses she prepares for them in the honey of her maternal sweetness and the unction of pure love. They then readily swallow them as they would sugared almonds, though the crosses may be very bitter. I believe that anyone who wishes to be devout and live piously in Jesus will suffer persecution (2Tim. 3:12) and will

have a daily cross to carry. But he will never manage to carry a heavy cross, or carry it joyfully and perseveringly, without a trusting devotion to our Lady, who is the very sweetness of the cross. It is obvious that a person could not keep on eating without great effort unripe fruit which has not been sweetened.

#155. 2) *This devotion is a short way to* discover Jesus, either because it is a road we do not wander from, or because, as we have just said, we walk along this road with greater ease and joy, and consequently with greater speed. We advance more in a brief period of submission of Mary and dependence on her than in whole years of self-will and self-reliance. A man who is obedient and submissive to Mary will sing of glorious victories over his enemies. It is true, his enemies will try to impede his progress, force him to retreat or try to make him fall. But with Mary's help, support and guidance, he will go forward towards our Lord. Without falling, retreating and even without being delayed, he will advance with giant strides towards Jesus along the same road which, as is written, Jesus took to come to us with giant strides and in a short time (Ps. 18:6).

#156. Why do you think our Lord spent only a few years here on earth and nearly all of them in submission and obedience to his Mother? The reason is that "attaining perfection in a short time, he lived a long time," (Wis. 4:13) even longer than Adam, whose losses he had come to make good. Yet Adam lived more than nine hundred years!

Jesus lived a long time, because he lived in complete submission to his Mother and in union with her, which obedience to God his Father required. The Holy Spirit tells us that the man who honors his mother is like a man who stores up a treasure. (Ecclus. 3:5) In other words, the man who honors Mary, his Mother, to the extent of subjecting himself to her and obeying her in all things will soon become very rich, because he is amassing riches every day through Mary who has become his secret philosopher's stone.

There is another quotation from Holy Scripture, *"My old age will be found in the mercy of the bosom."* According to the mystical interpretation of these words it is in the bosom of Mary that people who are young grow mature in enlightenment, in holiness, in experience and in wisdom, and in a short time reach the fullness of the age of Christ. For it was Mary's womb which encompassed and produced a perfect man. That same womb held the one whom the whole universe can neither encompass nor contain.

#157. 3) *This devotion is a perfect way* to reach our Lord and be united to him, for Mary is the most perfect and the most holy of all creatures, and Jesus, who came to us in a perfect manner, chose no other road for his great and wonderful journey. The Most High, the Incomprehensible One, the Inaccessible One, He who is, deigned to come down to us poor earthly creatures who are nothing at all. How was this done?

The Most High God came down to us in a perfect way through the humble Virgin Mary, without losing anything of his divinity or holiness. It is likewise through Mary that we poor creatures must ascend to almighty God in a perfect manner without having anything to fear.

God, the Incomprehensible, allowed himself to be perfectly comprehended and contained by the humble Virgin Mary without losing anything of his majesty. So it is also through Mary that we must draw near to God and unite ourselves to him perfectly, intimately, and without fear of being rejected.

Lastly, He who is deigned to come down to us who are not and turned our nothingness into God, or He who is. He did this perfectly by giving and submitting himself entirely to the young Virgin Mary without ceasing to be in time He who is from all eternity. Likewise it is through Mary that we, who are nothing, may become like God by grace and glory. We accomplish this by giving ourselves to her so perfectly and so completely as to remain nothing, as far as self is concerned, and to be everything in her, without any fear of illusion.

#158. Show me a new road to our Lord, pave it with all the merits of the saints, adorn it with their heroic virtues, illuminate and enhance it with the splendor and beauty of the angels, have all the angels and saints there to guide and protect those who wish to follow it. Give me such a road and truly, I boldly say, - and I am telling the truth - that instead of this road, perfect though it be, I would still choose the immaculate way of Mary. It is a way, a road without stain or spot, without original sin or actual sin, without shadow or darkness. When our loving Jesus comes in glory once again to reign upon earth - as he certainly will - he will choose no other way than the Blessed Virgin, by whom he came so surely and so perfectly the first time. The difference between his first and his second coming is that the first was secret and hidden, but the second will be glorious and resplendent. Both are perfect because both are through Mary.

Alas, this is a mystery which we cannot understand. *"Here let every tongue be silent."*

"Never will anyone who says the Rosary every day be will led astray. This is a statement that I would gladly sign with my blood."
St. Louis de Montfort

TWENTY-FOURTH DAY

Daily Prayers: *Litany of the Blessed Virgin, Ave Maris Stella, Prayer to Mary* and the *Holy Rosary.*

Daily Readings: Gospel of St. Luke 2:41-52 and True Devotion #'s 159-166.

Church Teaching For Further Reading: Catechism of the Catholic Church # 472.

Gospel of St. Luke 2:41-52 41. Now his parents went to Jerusalem every year at the feast of the Passover. 42. And when he was twelve years old, they went up according to custom; 43. and when the feast was ended, as they were returning, the boy Jesus stayed behind in Jerusalem. His parents did not know it, 44. but supposing him to be in the company they went a day's journey, and they sought him among their kinsfolk and acquaintances; 45. and when they did not find him, they returned to Jerusalem, seeking him. 46. After three days they found him in the temple, sitting among the teachers, listening to them and asking them questions; 47. and all who heard him were amazed at his understanding and his answers. 48. And when they saw him they were astonished; and his mother said to him, "Son, why have you treated us so? Behold, your father and I have been looking for you anxiously." 49. And he said to them, *"How is it that you sought me? Did you not know that I must be in my Father's house?"* And they did not understand the saying which he spoke to them. 51. And he went down with them and came to

Nazareth, and was obedient to them; and his mother kept all these things in her heart.

52. And Jesus increased in wisdom and in stature, and in favor with God and man.

True Devotion

#159. 4) *This devotion to our Lady is a sure way* to go to Jesus and to acquire holiness through union with him.

a) The devotion which I teach is not new. Its history goes back so far that the time of its origin cannot be ascertained with any precision, as Fr. Boudon, who died a short time ago in the odor of sanctity, states in a book which he wrote on this devotion. It is however certain that for more than seven hundred years we find traces of it in the Church.

St. Odilo, abbot of Cluny, who lived about the year 1040, was one of the first to practice it publicly in France as is told in his life.

Cardinal Peter Damian relates that in the year 1076 his brother, Blessed Marino, made himself the slave of the Blessed Virgin in the presence of his spiritual director in a most edifying manner. He placed a rope around his neck, scourged himself and placed on the altar a sum of money as a token of his devotion and consecration to our Lady. He remained so faithful to this consecration all his life that he merited to be visited and consoled on his deathbed by his dear Queen and hear from her lips the promise of paradise in reward for his service.

Caesarius Bollandus mentions a famous knight, Vautier de Birbak, a close relative of the Dukes of Louvain, who about the year 1300 consecrated himself to the Blessed Virgin.

This devotion was also practiced privately by many people up to the seventeenth century, when it became publicly known.

#160. Father Simon de Rojas of the order of the Holy Trinity for the Redemption of Captives, court preacher to Philip III, made this devotion popular throughout Spain and Germany. Through the intervention of Philip III, he obtained from Gregory XV valuable indulgences for those who practiced it.

Father de Los Rios of the order of St. Augustine, together with his intimate friend, Father de Rojas, worked hard, propagating it throughout Spain and Germany by preaching and writing. He composed a large volume entitled *Hierarchis Mariana,* where he treats of the antiquity, the excellence and the soundness of this devotion, with as much devotion as learning.

The Theatine Fathers in the seventeenth century established this devotion in Italy, Sicily and Savoy.

#161. Father Stanislaus Phalacius of the Society of Jesus spread this devotion widely in Poland.

Father de Los Rios in the book quoted above mentions the names of princes and princesses, bishops and cardinals of different countries who embraced this devotion.

Father Cornelius a Lapide, noted both for holiness and profound learning, was commissioned by several bishops and theologians to examine it. The praise he gave it after mature examination, is a worthy tribute to his own holiness. Many other eminent men followed his example.

The Jesuit Fathers, ever zealous in the service of our Blessed Lady, presented on behalf of the sodalities of Cologne to Duke Ferdinand of Bavaria, the then archbishop of Cologne, a little treatise on the devotion, and he gave it his approval and granted permission to have it printed. He exhorted all priests and religious of his diocese to do their utmost to spread this solid devotion.

#162. Cardinal de Berulle, whose memory is venerated throughout France, was outstandingly zealous in furthering the devotion in France, despite the calumnies and persecution he suffered at the hands of critics and evil men. They accused him of introducing novelty and superstition. They composed and published a libelous tract against him and they - or rather the devil in them - used a thousand stratagems to prevent him from spreading the devotion in France. But this eminent and saintly man responded to their calumnies with calm patience. He wrote a little book in reply to their libel and forcefully refuted the objections contained in it. He pointed out that this devotion is founded on the example given by Jesus Christ, on the obligations we have towards him and on the promises we made in holy baptism. It was mainly this last reason which silenced his enemies. He made clear to them that this consecration to the Blessed Virgin, and through her to Jesus, is nothing less than a perfect renewal of the promises and vows of baptism. He said many beautiful things concerning this devotion which can be read in his works.

#163. In Fr. Boudon's book we read of the different popes who gave their approval to this devotion, the theologians who examined it, the hostility it encountered and overcame, the thousands who made it their own without censure from any pope. Indeed it could not be condemned without overthrowing the foundations of Christianity.

It is obvious then that this devotion is not new. If it is not commonly practiced, the reason is that it is too sublime to be appreciated and undertaken by everyone.

#164. b) This devotion is a safe means of going to Jesus Christ, because it is Mary's role to lead us safely to her Son; just as it is the role of our Lord to lead us to the eternal Father. Those who are spiritually-minded should not fall into the error of thinking that Mary hinders our union with God. How could this possibly happen? How could Mary, who found grace with God for everyone in general and each one in particular, prevent a soul from obtaining the supreme grace of union with him?

It is quite true that the example of other people, no matter how holy, can sometimes impair union with God, but not so our Blessed Lady, as I have said and shall never weary of repeating. One reason why so few souls come to the fullness of the age of Jesus is that Mary who is still as much as ever his Mother and the fruitful spouse of the Holy Spirit is not formed well enough in their hearts. If we desire a ripe and perfectly formed fruit, we must posses the tree that bears it. If we desire the fruit of life, Jesus Christ, we must posses the tree of life which is Mary. If we desire to have the Holy Spirit working within us, we must possess his faithful and inseparable spouse, Mary, whom as I have said elsewhere, he can make fruitful.

#165. Rest assured that the more you turn to Mary in your prayers, meditations, actions and sufferings, seeing her if not perhaps clearly and distinctly, at least in a general and indistinct way, the more surely will you discover Jesus. For he is always greater, more powerful, more active and more mysterious when acting through Mary than he is in any other creature in the universe, or even in heaven. Thus Mary, so divinely-favored and so lost in God, is far from being an obstacle to good people who are striving for union with him. There has never been and there never will be a creature so ready to help us in achieving that union more effectively, for she will dispense to us all the graces to attain that end. As a saint once remarked, *"Only Mary knows how to fill our minds with the thought of God."* Moreover Mary will safeguard us against the deception and cunning of the evil one.

#166. Where Mary is present, the evil one is absent. One of the unmistakable signs that a person is led by the spirit of God is the devotion he has to Mary, and his habit of thinking and speaking of her. This is the opinion of a saint, who goes on to say that just as breathing is a proof that the body is not dead, so the habitual thought of Mary and loving converse with her is a proof that the soul is not spiritually dead in sin.

"Have you strayed from the path leading to heaven? Then call on Mary, for her name means 'Star of the Sea, the North Star which guides the ships of our souls during the voyage of this life,' and she will guide you to the harbor of eternal salvation."

St. Louis de Montfort

TWENTY-FIFTH DAY

Daily Prayers: *Litany of the Blessed Virgin, Ave Maris Stella, Prayer to Mary* and the *Holy Rosary.*

Daily Readings: Gospel of St. John 19:25-30 and True Devotion #'s 167-174.

Church Teaching For Further Reading: Catechism of the Catechism of the Catholic Church #'s 726, 2618, 501, 964, 2679.

Gospel of St. John 19:25-30 25. So the soldiers did this. But standing by the cross of Jesus were his mother and his mother's sister, Mary the wife of Clopas, and Mary Magdalene. 26. When Jesus saw his mother, and the disciple whom he loved standing near, he said to his mother, *"Woman, behold, you son!"* 27. Then he said to the disciple, *"Behold, your mother!"* And from that hour the disciple took her to his own home.

28. After this Jesus, knowing that all was now finished, said (to fulfill the scripture), *"I thirst."* 29. A bowl of vinegar stood there; so they put a sponge full of the vinegar on hyssop and held it to his mouth. 30. When Jesus had received the vinegar, he said, *"It is finished";* and he bowed his head and gave up his spirit.

True Devotion

#167. Since Mary alone has crushed all heresies, as we are told by the Church under the guidance of the Holy Spirit, (Office of B.V.M.), a devoted servant of hers will never fall into formal heresy or error, though critics may contest this. He may very well err

materially, mistaking lies for truth or an evil spirit for a good one, but he will be less likely to do this than others. Sooner or later he will discover his error and will not go on stubbornly believing and maintaining what he mistakenly thought was the truth.

#168. Whoever then wishes to advance along the road to holiness and be sure of encountering the true Christ, without fear of the illusions which afflict many devout people, should take up "with valiant heart and willing spirit" (2Macc. 1:3) this devotion to Mary which perhaps he had not heard about. Even if it is new to him, let him enter upon this excellent way which I am now revealing to him, "I will show you a more excellent way" (1Cor. 12:31).

It was opened up by Jesus Christ, the Incarnate Wisdom. He is our one and only Head, and we, his members, cannot go wrong in following him. It is a *smooth* way made easy by the fullness of grace, the unction of the Holy Spirit. In our progress along this road, we do not weaken or turn back. It is a *quick* way and leads us to Jesus in a short time. It is a *perfect* way without mud or dust or any vileness of sin. Finally, it is a reliable way, for it is *direct* and *sure,* having no turnings to right or left but leading us straight to Jesus and to life eternal.

Let us then take this road and travel along it night and day until we arrive at the fullness of the age of Jesus Christ.

6. *It gives liberty of spirit*

#169. This devotion gives great liberty of spirit - the freedom of the children of God - to those who faithfully practice it. Through

this devotion we make ourselves slaves of Jesus by consecrating ourselves entirely to him. To reward us for this enslavement of love, our Lord frees us from every scruple and servile fear which might restrict, imprison or confuse us; he opens our hearts and fills them with holy confidence in God, helping us to regard God as our Father; he inspires us with a generous and filial love.

#170. Without stopping to prove this truth, I shall simply relate an incident which I read in the life of Mother Agnes of Jesus, a Dominican nun of the convent of Langeac in Auvergne, who dies there in the odor of sanctity in 1634.

When she was only seven years old and was suffering great spiritual anguish, she heard a voice telling her that if she wished to be delivered from her anguish and protected against all her enemies, she should make herself the slave of our Lord and his Blessed Mother as soon as possible. No sooner had she returned home than she gave herself completely to Jesus and Mary as their slave, although she had never known anything about this devotion before. She found an iron chain, put it round her waist and wore it till the day she died. After this, all her sufferings and scruples disappeared and she found great peace of soul.

This led her to teach this devotion to many others who made rapid progress in it - among them, Fr. Olier, the founder of the Seminary of St. Sulpice, and several other priests and students from the same seminary. One day the Blessed Virgin appeared to Mother Agnes and put a gold chain around her neck to show her how happy she was that Mother Agnes had become the slave of both her and her Son. And St. Cecilia, who accompanied our Lady, said to her,

"Happy are the faithful slaves of the Queen of heaven, for they will enjoy true freedom." Tibi servire libertas.

7. It is of great benefit to our neighbor

#171. By this devotion we show love for our neighbor in an outstanding way, since we give him through Mary's hands all that we prize most highly - that is, the satisfactory and prayer value of all our good works, down to the least good thought and the least little suffering. We give our consent that all we have already acquired or will acquire until death should be used in accordance with our Lady's will for the conversion of sinners or the deliverance of souls from purgatory.

Is this not perfect love of our neighbor? Is this not being a true disciple of our Lord, one who should always be recognized by his love? Is this not the way to convert sinners without any danger of vainglory, and deliver souls from purgatory by doing hardly anything more than what we are obliged to do by our state of life?

#172. To appreciate the excellence of this motive we must understand what a wonderful thing it is to convert a sinner or to deliver a soul from purgatory. It is an infinite good, greater than the creation of heaven and earth, since it gives a soul the possession of God. If by this devotion we secured the release of only one soul from purgatory or converted only one sinner in our whole lifetime, would that not be enough to induce any person who really loves his neighbor to practice this devotion?

It must be noted that our good works, passing through Mary's hands, are progressively purified. Consequently, their merit and their satisfactory and prayer value is also increased. That is why they become much more effective in relieving the souls in purgatory and converting sinners than if they did not pass through the virginal and liberal hands of Mary. Stripped of self-will and clothed with disinterested love, the little that we give to the Blessed Virgin is truly powerful enough to appease the anger of God and draw down his mercy. It may well be that at the hour of death a person who has been faithful to this devotion will find that he has freed many souls from purgatory and converted many sinners, even though he performed only the ordinary actions of his state of life. Great will be his joy at the judgment. Great will be his glory throughout eternity.

8. *It is a wonderful means of perseverance*

#173. Finally, what draws us in a sense more compellingly to take up this devotion to the most Blessed Virgin is the fact that it is a wonderful means of persevering in the practice of virtue and of remaining steadfast.

Why is it that most conversions of sinners are not lasting? Why do they relapse so easily into sin? Why is it that most of the faithful, instead of making progress in one virtue after another and to acquiring new graces, often lose the little grace and virtue they have? This misfortune arises, as I have shown, for the fact that man, so prone to evil, so weak and changeable, trusts himself too much, relies on his own strength, and wrongly presumes he is able to safeguard his precious graces, virtues and merits.

By this devotion we entrust all we possess to Mary, the faithful Virgin. We choose her as the guardian of all our possessions in the natural and supernatural sphere. We trust her because she is faithful, we rely on her strength, we count on her mercy and charity to preserve and increase our virtues and merits in spite of the efforts of the devil, the world, and the flesh to rob us of them. We say to her as a good child would say to its mother or a faithful servant to the mistress of the house, "My dear Mother and Mistress, I realize that up to now I have received from God through your intercession more graces than I deserve. But bitter experience has taught me that I carry these riches in a very fragile vessel and that I am too weak and sinful to guard them by myself. Please accept in trust everything I possess, and in your faithfulness and power keep it for me. If you watch over me, I shall lose nothing. If you support me, I shall not fall. If you protect me, I shall be safe from my enemies.

#174. This is exactly what St. Bernard clearly pointed out to encourage us to take up this devotion. *"When Mary supports you, you will not fall. With her as your protector, you will have nothing to fear. With her as your guide you will not grow weary. When you win her favor, you will reach the port of heaven."* St. Bonaventure seems to say the same thing in even more explicit terms, *"The Blessed Virgin,"* he says, *not only preserves the fullness enjoyed by the saints, but she maintains the saints in their fullness so that it does not diminish. She prevents their virtues from fading away, their merits from being wasted and their graces from being lost. She prevents the*

devils from doing them harm and she so influences them that her divine Son has no need to punish them when they sin."

"If you say the Rosary faithfully unto death, I do assure you that, in spite of the gravity of your sins, 'you will receive a never fading crown of glory."

St. Louis de Montfort

TWENTY-SIXTH DAY

Daily Prayers: *Litany of the Blessed Virgin, Ave Maris Stella, Prayer to Mary* and the *Holy Rosary.*

Daily Readings: Revelation 11:19-12:1-6 and True Devotion #'s 175-182.

Church Teaching For Further Reading: Catechism of the Catholic Church #'s 1138-39.

Revelation 11:19-12:1-6 19. The God's temple in heaven was opened, and the ark of his covenant was seen within his temple; and there were flashes of lightning, loud noises, peals of thunder, and earthquake, and heavy hail.

12. And a great portent appeared in heaven, a woman clothed with the sun, with the moon under her feet, and on her head a crown of twelve stars; 2. she was with child and she cried out in her pangs of birth, in anguish for delivery. 3. And another portent appeared in heaven; behold, a great red dragon, with seven heads and ten horns, and seven diadems upon his heads. 4. His tail swept down a third of the stars of heaven, and cast them to the earth. And the dragon stood before the woman who was about to bear a child, the he might devour her child when she brought it forth; 5. she brought forth a male child, one who is to rule all the nations with a rod of iron, but her child was caught up to God and to his throne, 6. and the woman fled into the wilderness, where she has a place prepared by God, in which to be nourished for one thousand two hundred and sixty days.

True Devotion

#175. Mary is the Virgin most faithful who by her fidelity to God makes good the losses caused by Eve's unfaithfulness. She obtains fidelity to God and final perseverance for those who commit themselves to her. For this reason St. John Damascene compared her to a firm anchor which holds them fast and saves them from shipwreck in the raging seas of the world where so many people perish through lack of such a firm anchor. *"We fasten souls,"* he said, *"to Mary, our hope, as to a firm anchor."* It was to Mary that the saints who attained salvation most firmly anchored themselves as did others who wanted to ensure their perseverance in their holiness.

Blessed, indeed, are those Christians who bind themselves faithfully and completely to her as to a secure anchor! The violent storms of the world will not make them founder or carry away their heavenly riches. Blessed are those who enter into her as into another Noah's ark! The flood waters of sin which engulf so many will not harm them because, as the Church makes Mary say in the words of divine Wisdom, *"Those who work with my help - for their salvation - shall not sin."* Blessed are the unfaithful children of unhappy Eve who commit themselves to Mary, the ever-faithful Virgin and Mother who never wavers in her fidelity and never goes back on her trust. She always loves those who love her, not only with deep affection, but with a love that is active and generous. By an abundant outpouring of grace she keeps them from relaxing their effort in the practice of virtue or falling by the wayside through loss of divine grace.

#176. Moved by pure love, this good Mother always accepts whatever is given her in trust, and, once she accepts something, she binds herself in justice by a contract of trusteeship to keep it safe. Is not someone to whom I entrust the sum of a thousand francs obliged to keep it safe for me so that if it were lost through his negligence he would be responsible for it in strict justice? But nothing we entrust to the faithful Virgin will ever be lost through her negligence. Heaven and earth would pass away sooner than Mary would neglect or betray those who trusted in her.

#177. Poor children of Mary, you are extremely weak and changeable. Your human nature is deeply impaired. It is sadly true that you have been fashioned from the same corrupted nature as the other children of Adam and Eve. But do not let that discourage you. Rejoice and be glad! Here is a secret which I am revealing to you, a secret unknown to most Christians, even the most devout.

Do not leave your gold and silver in your own safes which have already been broken into and rifled many times by the evil one. They are too small, too flimsy and too old to contain such great and priceless possessions. Do not put pure and clear water from the spring into vessels fouled and infected by sin. Even if sin is no longer there, its odor persists and the water would be contaminated. You do not put choice wine into old casks that have contained sour wine. You would spoil the good wine and run the risk of losing it.

#178. Chosen souls, although you may already understand me, I shall express myself still more clearly. Do not commit the gold of your charity, the silver of your purity to a threadbare sack or a battered old chest, or the waters of heavenly grace or the wines of

your merits and virtues to a tainted and fetid cask, such as you are. Otherwise you will be robbed by thieving devils who are on the lookout day and night waiting for a favorable opportunity to plunder. If you do so, all those pure gifts from God will be spoiled by the unwholesome presence of self-love, inordinate self-reliance and self-will.

Pour into the bosom and heart of Mary all your precious possessions, all your graces and virtues. She is a spiritual vessel, a vessel of honor, a singular vessel of devotion. Ever since God personally hid himself with all his perfection in this vessel, it has become completely spiritual, and the spiritual abode of all spiritual souls. It has become honorable and has been the throne of honor for the greatest saints in heaven. It has become outstanding in devotion and the home of renowned for gentleness, grace and virtue. Moreover, it has become as rich as a house of gold, as strong as a tower of David and as pure as a tower of ivory.

#179. Blessed is the man who has given everything to Mary, who at all times and in all things trusts in her, and loses himself in her. He belongs to Mary and Mary belongs to him. With David he can boldly say, "She was created for me," or with the beloved disciple, "I have taken her for my own", or with the Lord himself, "All that is mine is yours and all that is yours is mine".

#180. If any critic reading this should imagine that I am exaggerating or speaking from an excess of devotion, he has not, alas, understood what I have said. Either he is a carnal man who has no taste for the spiritual; or he is a worldly man who has cut himself off from the Holy Spirit; or he is a proud and critical man who

ridicules and condemns anything he does not understand. But those who are born not of blood, nor of flesh, nor of the will of man, but of God and of Mary, understand and appreciate what I have to say. It is for them that I am writing.

#181. Nevertheless after this digression, I say to both the critics and the devout that the Blessed Virgin, the most reliable and generous of all God's creatures, never lets herself be surpassed by anyone in love and generosity. For the little that is given to her, she gives generously of what she has received from God. Consequently, if a person gives himself to her without reserve, she gives herself also without reserve to that person provided his confidence in her is not presumptuous and he does his best to practice virtue and curb his passions.

#182. So the faithful servants of the Blessed Virgin may confidently say with St. John Damascene, *"If I confide in you, Mother of God, I shall be saved. Under your protection I shall fear nothing. With your help I shall rout all my enemies. For devotion to you is a weapon of salvation which God gives to those he wishes to save." (Joan. Damas. Ser. De Annuntiat).*

"The Most Holy Virgin in these last times in which we live has given a new efficacy to the recitation of the Rosary to such an extent that there is no problem, no matter how difficult it is, whether temporal or above all spiritual, in the personal life of each one of us, of our families... that cannot be solved by the Rosary. There is no problem, I tell you, no matter how difficult it is, that we cannot resolve by the prayer of the Holy Rosary."

Sister Lucia dos Santos, Fatima seer

Fourth Period Theme
Knowledge of Jesus Christ

Next Seven Days

During the third week they should apply themselves to the study of Jesus Christ. They can meditate upon what we have said about Him, and say the prayer of Saint Augustine which they will find in this manual. They can, with the same saint, repeat a hundred times a day: "Lord, that I may know thee!" or "Lord, that I may see Who Thou art!"

What is to be studied in Christ? First the Man-God, His grace and glory; then His rights to sovereign dominion over us; since, after having renounced Satan and the world, we have taken Jesus Christ for our Lord. What next shall be the object of our study? His exterior actions and also His interior life; namely, the virtues and acts of His Sacred Heart: His association with Mary in the mysteries of the Annunciation and Incarnation, during His infancy and hidden life, at the feast of Cana and on Calvary.

Daily Prayers: *Ave Maris Stella, Litany of the Holy Name of Jesus or Litany of the Sacred Heart. Saint Louis De Montfort's prayer to Jesus, O Jesus Living in Mary,* and the *Payer of Saint Augustine* and the *Holy Rosary.*

Spiritual Exercises during the Third Week are: Acts of love of God to Jesus through Mary, thanksgiving for the blessings of Jesus, contrition for our sins and make resolutions on how to avoid and overcome our sins.

Mary Assumed Body and Soul Into Heaven

The next seven days, of the Knowledge of Jesus Christ, will be dedicated to the Blessed Mother's glorious Assumption of her body and soul into heaven. This *de fide* dogma was defined by Pope Pius XII in 1950 in *Munificentissimus Deus*. Pope Pius XII stated, "The Immaculate Mother of God, that ever Virgin Mary, having completed the course of her earthly life, was assumed body and soul into heavenly glory." After the Blessed Mother had died, wishing to pattern her life after that of her Son, her body remained miraculously incorrupt until her body was reunited with her soul. She now enjoys the beatific vision and there reigns with Jesus her Son as Queen of heaven and earth. The Blessed Mother now reigning as Queen is a natural consequence that flows from her being the Mother of God and the rest of her prerogatives that flowed from it. Let us say with St. Louis De Montfort and St. Catherine La Boure, "When will the Blessed Mother be proclaimed Queen of heaven and earth?" I would like to add, when will be she reign as Queen of all hearts?!

For further reading about the Assumption of the Blessed Mother, read the Catechism of the Catholic Church #'s 966, 974.

The support for this dogma found in Sacred Scripture is Genesis 3:15; Revelation 11:19.

TWENTY-SEVENTH DAY

Daily Prayers: *Ave Maris Stella, Litany of the Holy Name of Jesus or Litany of the Sacred Heart, Saint Louis De Montfort's prayer to Jesus, O Jesus Living in Mary, Prayer of Saint Augustine* and the *Holy Rosary.*

Daily Readings: Gospel of St. John 1:1-18 and True Devotion #'s 12, 13, 213.

Church Teaching For Further Reading: Catechism of the Catholic Church #'s 241, 291, 254-56, 242, 1997, 2780-82, 423, 456-63, 214, 697.

Gospel of St. John 1:1-18 In the beginning was the Word, and the Word was with God, and the Word was God. 2. He was in the beginning with God; 3. all things were made through him, and without him was not anything made that was made. 4. In him was life, and the life was the light of men. 5. The light shines in the darkness, and the darkness has not overcome it.

6. There was a man sent from God, whose name was John. 7. He came for testimony, to bear witness to the light, that all might believe through him. 8. He was not the light, but came to bear witness to the light. 9. The true light that enlightens every man was coming into the world. 10. He was in the world, and the world was made through him, yet the world knew him not. 11. He came to his own home, and his own people received him not. 12. But to all who received him, who believed in his name, he gave power to become

children of God; 13. who were born, not of blood nor of the will of the flesh nor of the will of man, but of God.

14. And the Word became flesh and dwelt among us, full of grace and truth; we have beheld his glory, glory as of the only Son from the Father. 15. (John bore witness to him, and cried, "This was he of whom I said, 'He who comes after me ranks before me, for he was before me.'") 16. And from his fullness have we all received, grace upon grace. 17. For the law was given through Moses; grace and truth came through Jesus Christ. 18. No one has ever seen God; the only Son, who is in the bosom of the Father, he has made him known.

True Devotion

#12. Finally, we must say in the words of the apostle Paul, "Eye has not seen, nor has ear heard, nor has the heart of man understood" (1Cor. 2:9) the beauty, the grandeur, the excellence of Mary, who is indeed a miracle of miracles of grace, nature and glory. "If you wish to understand the mother," says a saint, "then understand the Son. She is a worthy Mother of God". *Hic tacit omnis lingua:* Here let every tongue be silent.

#13. My heart has dictated with special joy all that I have written to show that Mary has been unknown up till now, and that this is one of the reasons why Jesus Christ is not known as he should be. If then, as is certain, the knowledge and the kingdom of Jesus Christ must come into the world, it can only be as a necessary consequences of the knowledge and reign of Mary. She who first gave him to the world will establish his kingdom in the world.

WONDERFUL EFFECTS OF THIS DEVOTION

#213. My dear friend, be sure that if you remain faithful to the interior and exterior practices of this devotion which I will point out, the following effects will be produced in your soul:

1. Knowledge of our unworthiness

By the light which the Holy Spirit will give you through Mary, his faithful spouse, you will perceive the evil inclinations of your fallen nature and how incapable you are of any good apart from that which God produces in you as Author of nature and of grace. As a consequence of this knowledge you will despise yourself and think of yourself only as an object of repugnance. You will consider yourself as a snail that soils everything with its slime, as a toad that poisons everything with its venom, as a malevolent serpent seeking only to deceive. Finally, the humble Virgin Mary will share her humility with you so that, although you regard yourself with distaste and desire to be disregarded by others, you will not look down slightingly upon anyone.

"Mary may be truly called the Stairway of Heaven. By her God descended from heaven to the world so that by her we might ascend from earth to heaven."
St. Fulgentius

TWENTY-EIGHTH DAY

Daily Prayers: *Ave Maris Stella*, Litany of the Holy Name of Jesus or Litany of the Sacred Heart, St. Louis De Montfort's prayer to Jesus, *O Jesus Living in Mary*, a *Prayer of St. Augustine* and the *Holy Rosary*.

Daily Readings: Gospel of St. John 6:22-71 and True Devotion #'s 214-216.

Church Teaching For Further Reading: Catechism of the Catholic Church #'s 1094, 161, 1381, 475, 2824, 1391, 1331, 737, 1336.

Gospel of St. John 6:22-71 22. On the next day the people who remained on the other side of the sea saw that there had been only one boat there, and that Jesus had not entered the boat with his disciples, but that his disciples had gone away alone. 23. However, boats from Tiberias came near the place where they ate the bread after the Lord had given thanks. 24. So when the people saw that Jesus was not there, nor his disciples, they themselves got into the boats and went to Capernaum, seeking Jesus. 25. When they found him on the other side of the sea, they said to him, "Rabbi, when did you come here?" 26. Jesus answered them, *"Truly, truly, I say to you, you seek me, not because you saw signs, but because you ate your fill of the loaves. 27. Do not labor for the food which perishes, but for the food which endures to eternal life, which the Son of man will give to you; for on him has God the Father set his seal."* 28. Then they said to him, "What must we do, to be doing the works of God?" 29. Jesus answered them, *"This is the work of God, that you* believe in him whom he has sent." 30. So they said to him, "Then what sign do you do, that we may see, and believe you? What work do you perform? 31. Our fathers ate the manna in the wilderness; as it is written, 'He gave them bread from heaven to eat.'" 32. Jesus then said to them, *"Truly, truly, I say to you, it was not Moses who gave you the bread from heaven; my father gives you the true bread from heaven. 33. For the bread of God is that which comes down from heaven, and gives life to the world."* 34. They said to him, "Lord, give us this bread always."

35. Jesus said to them, *"I am the bread of life; he who comes to me shall not hunger, and he who believes in me shall never thirst. 36. But I said to you that you have seen me and yet do not believe. 37. All that the Father gives me will come to me; and him who comes to me I will not cast out. 38. For I have come down from heaven, not to do my own will, but the will of him who sent me; 39. and this is the will of him who sent me, that I should lose nothing of all that he has given me, but raise it up at the last day. 40. For this is the will of my Father, that every one who sees the Son and believes in him should have eternal life; and I will raise him up at the last day."*

41. The Jews then murmured at him, because he said, "I am the bread which come down from heaven." 42. They said, "Is not this Jesus, the son of Joseph, whose father and mother we know? How does he now say, 'I have come down from heaven'?" 43. Jesus answered them, *"Do not murmur among yourselves. 44. No one can come to me unless the Father who sent me draws him; and I will raise him up at the last day. 45. It is written in the prophets, 'And they shall all be taught by God.' Every one who has heard and*

learned from the Father comes to me. 46. Not that any one has seen the Father except him who is from God; he has seen the Father. 47. Truly, truly, I say to you, he who believes has eternal life. 48. I am the bread of life. 49. Your fathers ate the manna in the wilderness, and they died. 50. This is the bread which comes down from heaven, that a man may eat of it and not die. 51. I am the living bread which came down from heaven; if any one eats of this bread, he will live for ever; and the bread which I shall give for the life of the world is my flesh."

52. The Jews then disputed among themselves, saying, "How can this man give us his flesh to eat?" 53. So Jesus said to them, *"Truly, truly, I say to you, unless you eat the flesh of the Son of man and drink his blood, you have no life in you; 54. he who eats my flesh and drinks my blood has eternal life, and I will raise him up at the last day. 55. For my flesh is food indeed, and my blood is drink indeed. 56. He who eats my flesh and drinks my blood abides in me, and I in him. 57. As the living Father sent me, and I live because of the Father, so he who eats me will live because of me. 58. This is the bread which came down from heaven, not such as the fathers ate and died; he who eats this bread will live for ever."* 59. This he said in the synagogue, as he taught at Capernaum.

60. Many of his disciples, when they heard it, said, "This is a hard saying; who can listen to it?" 61. But Jesus, knowing in himself that his disciples murmured at it, said to them, *"Do you take offense at this? 62. Then what if you were to see the Son of man ascending where he was before? 63. It is the spirit that gives life, the flesh is of no avail; the words that I have spoken to you are spirit and life. 64.*

But there are some of you that do not believe." For Jesus knew from the first who those were that did not believe, and who it was that should betray him. 65. And he said, *"This is why I told you that no one can come to me unless it is granted him by the Father."*

66. After this many of his disciples drew back and no longer went about with him. 67. Jesus said to the twelve, *"Will you also go away?"* 68. Simon Peter answered him, "Lord, to whom shall we go? You have the words of eternal life; 69. and we have believed, and have come to know that you are the Holy One of God." 70. Jesus answered them, *"Did I not choose you, the twelve, and one of you is a devil?"* 71. He spoke of Judas the son of Simon Iscariot, for he, one of the twelve, was to betray him.

True Devotion

2. A Share in Mary's Faith

#214. Mary will share her faith with you. Her faith on earth was stronger than that of all the patriarchs, prophets, apostles and saints. Now that she is reigning in heaven she no longer has this faith, since she sees everything clearly in God by the light of glory. However, with the consent of Almighty God she did not lose it when entering heaven. She has preserved it for her faithful servants in the Church Militant. Therefore the more you gain the friendship of this noble Queen and Virgin, the more will you be inspired by faith in your daily life. It will cause you to depend less upon sensible and extraordinary feelings. For it is a lively faith animated by charity enabling you to do everything from no other motive than that of pure love. (This number is filled with biblical allusion: Gal. 5:6; Col. 1:23; Rom. 5:1-2; Heb. 11:33; Col. 2:3; Lk. 1:79; 1Pet. 5:8-9) It is a firm faith, unshakeable as a rock, prompting you to remain firm and steadfast in the midst of storms and tempests. It is an active and probing faith which like some mysterious pass-key admits you into the mysteries of Jesus Christ and of man's final destiny and into the very heart of God himself. It is a courageous faith which inspires you to undertake and carry out without hesitation great things for God and the salvation of souls. Lastly, this faith will be your flaming torch, your very life with God your secret fund of divine Wisdom, and an all-powerful weapon for you to enlighten those who sit in darkness and the shadow of death. It inflames those who are lukewarm and need the gold of fervent love. It restores life to those who are dead through sin. It moves and transforms hearts of marble and cedars of Lebanon by gentle and convincing argument. Finally, this faith will strengthen you to resist the devil and the other enemies of salvation.

3. The gift of pure love

#215. The Mother of fair love will rid your heart of all scruples and inordinate servile fear. She will open and enlarge it to obey the commandments of her Son with alacrity and with the holy freedom of the children of God. She will fill your heart with pure love of which she is the treasury. You will then cease to act, as you did before, out of fear of God who is love, but rather out of pure love.

You will look upon him as a loving Father and endeavor to please him at all times. You will speak trustfully to him as a child does to its father. If you should have the misfortune to offend him you will abase yourself before him and humbly beg his pardon. You will offer your hand to him with simplicity and lovingly rise from your sin. Then, peaceful and relaxed and buoyed up with hope, you will continue on your way to him.

4. Great confidence in God and in Mary

#216. Our Blessed Lady will fill you with unbounded confidence in God and in herself:

1) Because you will no longer approach Jesus by yourself but always through Mary your loving Mother.

2) Since you have given her all your merits, graces and satisfactions to dispose of as she pleases, she imparts to you her own virtues and clothes you in her own merits. So you will be able to say confidently to God, "Behold Mary, your handmaid, be it done unto me according to your word."

3) Since you have now given yourself completely to Mary, body and soul, she, who is generous to the generous, and more generous than even the kindest benefactor, will in return give herself to you in a marvelous but real manner. Indeed you may without hesitation say to her, "I am yours, O Blessed Virgin, obtain salvation for me", (Ps. 118:94) or with the beloved disciple, St. John, "I have taken you, Blessed Mother, for my all." Or again you may say with St. Bonaventure, "Dear Mother of saving grace, I will do everything

with confidence and without fear because you are my strength and my boast in the Lord," or in another place, "I am yours and all that I have is yours, O glorious Virgin blessed above all created things. Let me place you as a seal upon my heart, for your love is as strong as death." Or adopting the sentiments of the prophet, "Lord, my heart has no reason to be exalted nor should my looks be proud; I have not sought things of great moment nor wonders beyond my reach, nevertheless, I still am not humble. But I have roused my soul and taken courage. I am as a child, weaned from earthly pleasures and resting on its mother's breast. It is upon this breast that all good things come to me." (Ps. 130:1-2)

4) What will still further increase your confidence in her is that, after having given her in trust all that you possess to use or keep as she pleases, you will place less trust in yourself and much more in her whom you have made your treasury. How comforting and how consoling when a person can say that the treasury of God, where he has placed all that he holds most precious, is also his treasury. "She is," says a saintly man, "the treasury of the Lord."

"One day through the Rosary and the Scapular,
Our Lady will save the world."

St. Dominic

TWENTY-NINETH DAY

Daily Prayers: Ave Maris Stella, Litany of the Holy Name of Jesus, or Litany of the Sacred Heart, St. Louis De Montfort's prayer to Jesus, O Jesus Living in Mary, Prayer of St. Augustine and the *Holy Rosary.*

Daily Readings: Gospel of St. John 10:1-18 and True Devotion #'s 217-219.

Church Teaching For Further Reading: Catechism of the Catholic Church #'s 609, 553, 754, 813-22, 609.

Gospel of St. John 10:1-18 *"Truly, truly, I say to you, he who does not enter the sheepfold by the door but climbs in by another way, that man is a thief and a robber; 2. but he who enters by the door is the shepherd of the sheep. 3. To him the gatekeeper opens; the sheep hear his voice, and he calls his own sheep by name and leads them out. 4. When he has brought out all his own, he goes before them, and the sheep follow him, for they know his voice. 5. A stranger they will not follow, but they will flee from him, for they do not know the voice of strangers."* 6. This figure Jesus used with them, but they did not understand what he was saying to them.

7. So Jesus again said to them, *"Truly, truly, I say to you, I am the door of the sheep. 8. All who come before me are thieves and robbers; but the sheep did not heed them. 9. I am the door; if any one enters by me, he will be saved, and will go in and out and find pasture. 10. The thief comes only to steal and kill and destroy; I came that they may have life, and have it abundantly. 11. I am the*

good shepherd. The good shepherd lays down his life for the sheep. 12. He who is a hireling and not a shepherd, whose own the sheep are not, sees the wolf coming and leaves the sheep and flees; and the wolf snatches them and scatters them. 13. He flees because he is a hireling and cares nothing for the sheep. 14. I am the good shepherd; I know my own and my own know me, 15. as the Father knows me and I know the Father; and I lay down my life for the sheep. 16. And I have other sheep, that are not of this fold; I must bring them also, and they will heed my voice. So there shall be one flock, one shepherd. 17. For this reason the Father loves me, because I lay down my life, that I may take it again. 18. No one takes it from me, but I lay it down of my own accord. I have power to lay it down, and I have power to take it again; this charge I have received from my Father."

True Devotion

5. *Communication of the spirit of Mary*

#217. The soul of Mary will be communicated to you to glorify the Lord. Her spirit will take the place of yours to rejoice in God, her Savior, but only if you are faithful to the practices of this devotion. As St. Ambrose says, "May the soul of Mary be in each one of us to glorify the Lord! May the spirit of Mary be in each one of us to rejoice in God!" "When will that happy day come," asks a saintly man of our own day whose life was completely wrapped up in Mary, "when God's Mother is enthroned in men's hearts as Queen,

subjecting them to the dominion of her great and princely Son. When will souls breathe Mary as the body breathes air?

When that time comes wonderful things will happen on earth. The Holy Spirit, finding his dear Spouse present again in souls, will come down into them with great power. He will fill them with his gifts, especially wisdom, by which they will produce wonders of grace. My dear friends, when will that happy time come, that age of Mary, when many souls, chosen by themselves completely in the depths of her soul, becoming living copies of her, loving and glorifying Jesus. That day will dawn only when the devotion I teach is understood and put into practice. *Ut adveniat regnum tuum, adveniat regnum Mariae.* "Lord, that your kingdom may come, may the reign of Mary come!"

6. *Transformation into the likeness of Jesus*

#218. If Mary, the Tree of Life, is well cultivated in our soul by fidelity to this devotion, she will in due time bring forth her fruit, which is none other than Jesus. I have seen many devout souls searching for Jesus in one way or another, and so often when they have worked hard throughout the night, all they can say is, "Despite our having worked all night, we have caught nothing." (Lk. 5:5) To them we can say, "You have worked hard and gained little: (Hag. 1:6) Jesus can only be recognized faintly in you." But if we follow the immaculate path of Mary, living the devotion that I teach, we will always work in daylight, we will work in a holy place, and we will work but little. There is no darkness in Mary, not even the slightest shadow since there was never any sin in her. She is a holy place, a holy of holies, in which saints are formed and molded.

#219. Please note that I say that saints are molded in Mary. There is a vast difference between carving a statue by blows of hammer and chisel and making a statue by using a mold. Sculptors and statue-makers work hard and need plenty of time to make statues by the first method. But the second method does not involve much work and takes very little time. St. Augustine speaking to our Blessed Lady says, *"You are worthy to be called the mold of God."* Mary is a mold capable of forming people into the image of the God-man. Anyone who is cast into this divine mold is quickly shaped and molded into Jesus and Jesus into him. At little cost and in a short time he will become Christ-like since he is cast into the very same mold that fashioned a God-man.

"The love of the Immaculate is the most perfect love with which a creature can love God. With Her heart then let us strive to love the Heart of Jesus more and more. Let this be our greatest incentive."
St. Maximilian Kolbe

THIRTIETH DAY

Daily Prayers: *Ave Maris Stella*, Litany of the Holy Name of Jesus or Litany of the Sacred Heart, *St. Louis De Montfort's prayer to Jesus, O Jesus Living in Mary, Prayer of St. Augustine* and the *Holy Rosary*.

Daily Readings: Gospel of St. John 14:1-31 and True Devotion #'s 220-222.

Church Teaching For Further Reading: Catechism of the Catholic Church #'s 2795, 661, 2466, 516, 2614-15, 797, 788, 1380, 260, 243, 729, 606.

Gospel of St. John 14:1-31 *"Let not your hearts be troubled; believe in God, believe also in me. 2. In my Father's house are many rooms; if it were not so, would I have told you that I go to prepare a place for you? 3. And when I go and prepare a place for you, I will come again and will take you to myself, that where I am you may be also. 4. And you know the way where I am going."* 5. Thomas said to him, "Lord, we do not know where you are going; how can we know the way?" 6. Jesus said to him, *"I am the way, and the truth, and the life; no one comes to the Father, but by me. 7. If you had known me, you would have known my Father also; henceforth you know him and have seen him."*

8. Philip said to him, "Lord, show us the Father, and we shall be satisfied." 9. Jesus said to him, *"Have I been with you so long, and yet you do not know me, Philip? He who has seen me has seen the Father; how can you say, 'Show us the Father'? 10. Do you not*

believe that I am in the Father and the Father in me? The words that I say to you I do not speak on my own authority; but the Father who dwells in me does his works. 11. Believe me that I am in the Father and the Father in me; or else believe me for the sake of the works themselves.

12. "Truly, truly, I say to you, he who believes in me will also do the works that I do; and greater works than these will he do, because I go to the Father. 13. Whatever you ask in my name, I will do it, that the Father may be glorified in the Son; 14. if you ask anything in my name, I will do it.

15. "If you love me, you will keep my commandments. 16. And I will pray the Father, and he will give you another Counselor, to be with you forever, 17. even the Spirit of truth, whom the world cannot receive, because it neither sees him nor knows him; you know him, for he dwells with you, and will be in you.

18. "I will not leave you desolate; I will come to you. 19. Yet a little while, and the world will see me no more, but you will see me; because I live, you will live also. 20. In that day you will know that I am in my Father, and you in me, and I in you. 21. He who has my commandments and keeps them, he it is who loves me; and he who loves me will be loved by my Father, and I will love him and manifest myself to him." 22. Judas (not Iscariot) said to him, "Lord, how is it that you will manifest yourself to us, and not to the world?" 23. Jesus answered him, *"If a man loves me, he will keep my word, and my Father will love him, and we will come to him and make our home with him. 24. He who does not love me does not keep my words; and the word which you hear is not mine but the Father's who sent me.*

25. "These things I have spoken to you, while I am still with you. 26. But the Counselor, the Holy Spirit, whom the Father will send in my name, he will teach you all things, and bring to your remembrance all that I have said to you. 27. Peace I leave with you; my peace I give to you; not as the world gives do I give to you. Let not your hearts be troubled, neither let them be afraid. 28. You heard me say to you, 'I go away, and I will come to you.' If you loved me, you would have rejoiced, because I go to the Father; for the Father is greater than I. 29. And now I have told you before it takes place, so that when it does take place, you may believe. 30. I will no longer talk much with you, for the ruler of this world is coming. He has no power over me; 31. but I do as the Father has commanded me, so that the world may know that I love the Father. Rise let us go hence."

True Devotion

#220. I think I can very well compare to sculptors some spiritual directors and devout persons who wish to produce Jesus in themselves and in others by methods other than this. Many of them rely on their own skill, ingenuity and art, and chip away endlessly with mallet and chisel at hard stone or badly-prepared wood, in an effort to produce a likeness of our Lord. At times, they do not manage to produce a recognizable likeness either because they lack knowledge and experience of the person of Jesus or because a clumsy stroke has spoiled the whole work. But those who accept this little known secret of grace which I offer them can rightly be compared to smelters and molders who have discovered the beautiful

mold of Mary where Jesus was so divinely and so naturally formed. ("Naturally", that is in human nature and by voluntary collaboration. "Divinely", that is, by the operation of the Holy Spirit.)

They do not rely on their own skill but on the perfection of the mold. They cast and lose themselves in Mary where they become true models of her Son.

#221. You may think this is a beautiful and convincing comparison. But how many understand it? I would like you, my dear friend, to understand it. But remember **that only molten and liquefied substances may be poured into a mold. That means that you must crush and melt down the old Adam in you if you wish to acquire the likeness of the new Adam in Mary.**

7. *The greater glory of Christ*

#222. If you live this devotion sincerely, you will give more glory to Jesus in a month than in many years of a more demanding devotion. Here are my reasons for saying this:

1) Since you do everything through the Blessed Virgin as required by this devotion, you naturally lay aside your own intentions no matter how good they appear to you. You abandon yourself to our Lady's intentions even though you do not know what they are. Thus you share in the high quality of her intentions which are so pure that she gave more glory to God by the smallest of her actions, say, twirling her distaff or making a stitch, than did St. Laurence suffering his cruel martyrdom on the grid-iron, and even more than all the saints together in all their most heroic deeds! Mary amassed such a

multitude of merits and graces during her sojourn on earth that it would be easier to count the stars in heaven, the drops of water in the ocean or the sands of the sea-shore than count her merits and graces. She thus gave more glory to God than all the angels and saints have given or will ever give him. Mary, wonder of God, when souls abandon themselves to you, you cannot but work wonders in them!

> *"The Immaculate is the Omnipotent Beseecher*
> *Every conversion and sanctification is the work of grace,*
> *and She is the Mediatrix of All Graces.*
> *Since She Herself will suffice to beg and grant grace."*
> *St. Maximilian Kolbe*

THIRTY-FIRST DAY

Daily Prayers: Ave Maris Stella, Litany of the Holy Name of Jesus or Litany of the Sacred Heart, St. Louis De Montfort's prayer to Jesus, O Jesus Living in Mary, Prayer of St. Augustine and the Holy Rosary.

Daily Readings: Gospel of St. John 15:1-27 and True Devotion #'s 223-225.

Church Teaching For Further Reading: Catechism of the Catholic Church #'s 787, 737, 308, 2074, 244-48.

Gospel of St. John 15:1-27 *"I am the true vine, and my Father is the vinedresser. 2. Every branch of mine that bears no fruit, he takes away, and every branch that does bear fruit he prunes, that it may bear more fruit. 3. You are already made clean by the word which I have spoken to you. 4. Abide in me, and I in you. As the branch cannot bear fruit by itself, unless it abides in the vine, neither can you, unless you abide in me. 5. I am the vine, you are the branches. He who abides in me, and I in him, he it is that bears much fruit, for apart from me you can do nothing. 6. If a man does not abide in me, he is cast forth as a branch and withers; and the branches are gathered, thrown into the fire and burned. 7. If you abide in me, and my words abide in you, ask whatever you will, and it shall be done for you. 8. By this my Father is glorified, that you bear much fruit, and so prove to be my disciples. 9. As the Father has loved me, so have I loved you; abide in my love. 10. If you keep my commandments, you will abide in my love, just as I have kept my*

Father's commandments and abide in his love. 11. These things I have spoken to you, that my joy may be in you, and that your joy may be full.

12. "This is my commandment, that you love one another as I have loved you. 13. Greater love has no man than this, that a man lay down his life for his friends. 14. You are my friends if you do what I command you. 15. No longer do I call you servants, for the servant does not know what his master is doing; but I have called you friends, for all that I have heard from my Father I have made known to you. 16. You did not choose me, but I chose you and appointed you that you should go and bear fruit and that your fruit should abide; so that whatever you ask of the Father in my name, he may give it to you. 17. This I command you, to love one another.

18. "If the world hates you, know that it has hated me before it hated you. 19. If you were of the world, the world would love its own; but because you are not of the world, but I chose you out of the world, therefore the world hates you. 20. Remember the word that I said to you. 'A servant is not greater than his master.' If they persecuted me, they will persecute you; if they kept my word, they will keep yours also. 21. But all this they will do to you on my account, because they do not know him who sent me. 22. If I had not come and spoken to them, they would not have sin; but now they have no excuse for their sin. 23. He who hates me hates my Father also. 24. If I had not done among them the works which no one else did, they would not have sin; but now they have seen and hated both me and my Father. 25. It is to fulfill the word that is written in their law, 'They hated me without a cause.' 26. But when the Counselor

comes, whom I shall send to you from the Father, even the Spirit of truth, who proceeds from the Father, he will bear witness to me; 27. and you also are witnesses, because you have been with me from the beginning."

True Devotion

#223. 2) In this devotion we set no store on our own thoughts and actions but are content to rely on Mary's dispositions when approaching and even speaking to Jesus. We then act with far greater humility than others who, imperceptibly, rely on their own dispositions and are self-satisfied about them; and consequently we give greater glory to God, for perfect glory is given to him only by the lowly and humble of heart.

#224. 3) Our Blessed Lady, in her immense love for us, is eager to receive into her virginal hands the gift of our actions, imparting to them a marvelous beauty and splendor, and presenting them herself to Jesus most willingly. More glory is given to our Lord in this way than when we make our offering with our own guilty hands.

#225. 4) Lastly, you never think of Mary without Mary thinking of God for you. You never praise or honor Mary without Mary joining you in praising and honoring God. Mary is entirely relative to God. Indeed I would say that she was relative only to God, because she exists uniquely in reference to him. She is an echo of God, speaking and repeating only God. If you say "Mary" she says "God". When St. Elizabeth praised Mary calling her blessed because she had believed, Mary, the faithful echo of God, responded with her

Canticle, "My soul glorifies the Lord." What Mary did on that day, she does every day. When we praise her, when we love and honor her, when we present anything to her, then God is praised, honored and loved, and receives our gift through Mary and in Mary.

"The Rosary will cause virtue and good works to flourish;
it will obtain for souls the abundant mercy of God;
it will withdraw the hearts of men from the love of the world
and its vanities, and will lift them to the desire of eternal things.
Oh, that souls would sanctify themselves by this means."

Promises given to St. Dominic

THIRTY-SECOND DAY

Daily Prayers: *Ave Maris Stella, Litany of the Holy Name of Jesus or Litany of the Sacred Heart, St. Louis De Montfort's prayer, O Jesus Living in Mary, St. Augustine's Prayer* and the *Holy Rosary.*

Daily Readings: Gospel of St. Matthew 26:1-2, 26-29, 36-46; 27:36-44; Gospel of St. John 19:31-37 and True Devotion #'s 257-259.

Church Teaching For Further Reading: Catechism of the Catholic Church #'s 1328-29, 545, 610, 613, 1365, 1846, 2839, 1403, 2849, 363, 536, 612, 2719, 2733, 2846, 585, 1225, 608.

Gospel of St. Matthew 26:1-2, 26-29, 36-46 When Jesus had finished all these sayings, he said to his disciples, 2. *"You know that after two days the Passover is coming, and the Son of man will be delivered up to be crucified."*

26. Now as they were eating, Jesus took bread, and blessed, and broke it, and gave it to the disciples and said, *"Take, eat; this is by body."* 27. And he took a cup, and when he had given thanks he gave it to them, saying, *"Drink of it, all of you; 28. for this is my blood of the covenant, which is poured out for many for the forgiveness of sins. 29. I tell you I shall not drink again of this fruit of the vine until that day when I drink it new with you in my Father's kingdom."*

36. Then Jesus went with them to a place called Gethsemane, and he said to his disciples, *"Sit here, while I go yonder to pray."* 37. And taking with him Peter and the two sons of Zebedee, he began to be sorrowful and troubled. 38. Then he said to them, *"My soul is*

very sorrowful, even to death; remain here, and watch with me." 39. And going a little father he fell on his face and prayed, "My Father, if it be possible, let this cup pass from me; nevertheless, not as I will, but as thou wilt." 40. And he came to the disciples and found them sleeping; and he said to Peter, "So, could you not watch with me one hour? 41. Watch and pray that you may not enter into temptation; the spirit indeed is willing, but the flesh is weak." 42. Again, for the second time, he went away and prayed, "My Father, if this cannot pass unless I drink it, thy will be done." 43. And again he came and found them sleeping, for their eyes were heavy. 44. So, leaving them again, he went away and prayed for the third time, saying the same words. 45. Then he came to the disciples and said to them, "Are you still sleeping and taking your rest? Behold, the hour is at hand, and the Son of man is betrayed into the hands of sinners. 46. Rise, let us be going; see, my betrayer is at hand."

Gospel of St. Matthew 27:33-44   33. And when they came to a place called Golgotha (which means the place of a skull), 34. they offered him wine to drink, mingled with gall; but when he tasted it, he would not drink it. 35. And when they had crucified him, they divided his garments among them by casting lots; 36. then they sat down and kept watch over him there. 37. And over his head they put the charge against him, which read, "This is Jesus the King of the Jews." 38. Then two robbers were crucified with him, one on the right and one on the left. 39. And those who passed by derided him, wagging their heads 40. and saying, "You who would destroy the temple and build it in three days, save yourself! If you are the Son of

God, come down from the cross." 41. So also the chief priests, with the scribes, and elders, mocked him, saying, 42. "He saved others; he cannot save himself. He is the King of Israel; let him come down now from the cross, and we will believe in him. 43. He trusts in God; let God deliver him now, if he desires him; for he said, 'I am the Son of God.'" 44. And the robbers who were crucified with him also reviled him in the same way.

True Devotion

2. SPECIAL INTERIOR PRACTICES FOR THOSE WHO WISH TO BE PERFECT

#257. The exterior practices of this devotion which I have just dealt with should be observed as far as one's circumstances and state of life permit. They should not be omitted through negligence or deliberate disregard. In addition to them, here are some very sanctifying interior practices for those souls who feel called by the Holy Spirit to a high degree of perfection. They may be expressed in four words, doing everything THROUGH Mary, WITH Mary, IN Mary and FOR Mary, in order to do them more perfectly *through* Jesus, *with* Jesus, *in* Jesus, and *for* Jesus.

Through Mary

#258. We must do everything through Mary, that is, we must obey her always and be led in all things by her spirit, which is the

Holy Spirit of God. "Those who are let by the Spirit of God are children of God," says St. Paul. (Rom. 8:14) Those who are led by the spirit of Mary are children of Mary, and, consequently children of God, as we have already shown. Among the many servants of Mary only those who are truly and faithfully devoted to her are led by her spirit.

I have said that the spirit of Mary is the spirit of God because she was never led by her own spirit, but always by the spirit of God, who made himself master of her to such an extent that he became her very spirit. That is why St. Ambrose says, "May the spirit of Mary be in each one of us to rejoice in God." Happy is the man who follows the example of the good Jesuit Brother Rodriguez, who dies in the odor of sanctity, because he will be completely possessed and governed by the spirit of Mary, a spirit which is gentle yet strong, zealous yet prudent, humble yet courageous, pure yet fruitful.

#259. The person who wishes to be led by this spirit of Mary:

1) Should renounce his own spirit, his own views and his own will before doing anything, for example, before making meditation, celebrating or attending Mass, before Communion. For the darkness of our own spirit and the evil tendencies of our own will and actions, good as they may seem to us, would hinder the holy spirit of Mary were we to follow them.

2) We should give ourselves up to the spirit of Mary to be moved and directed as she wishes. We should place and leave ourselves in her virginal hands, like a tool in the hands of a craftsman or a lute in the hands of a good musician. We should cast ourselves into her like a stone thrown into the sea. This is done easily and

quickly by a mere thought, a slight movement of the will or just a few words as - "I renounce myself and give myself to you, my dear Mother." And even if we do not experience any emotional fervor in this spiritual encounter, it is none the less real. It is just as if a person with equal sincerity were to say - which God forbid! - "I give myself to the devil." Even though this were said without feeling any emotion, he would no less really belong to the devil.

3) From time to time during an action and after it, we should renew this same act of offering and of union. The more we do so, the quicker we shall grow in holiness and the sooner we shall reach union with Christ, which necessarily follows upon union with Mary, since the spirit of Mary is the spirit of Jesus.

"Just as she alone is greater than all the angels and saints together, so is she more solicitous for us than them all."

St. Augustine

THIRTY-THIRD DAY

Daily Prayers: *Ave Maris Stella, Litany of the Holy Name of Jesus or Litany of the Sacred Heart of Jesus, St. Louis De Montfort's Prayer, O Jesus Living in Mary, St. Augustine's Prayer* and the *Holy Rosary.*

Daily Readings: Gospel of St. John 19:26-37; 20:19-23 and True Devotion #'s 260-265.

Church Teaching For Further Reading: Catechism of the Catholic Church #'s 585, 1225, 608, 645, 1116, 553, 730, 976, 1441, 1461.

Gospel of St. John 19:26-37 *26.* When Jesus saw his mother, and the disciple whom he loved standing near, he said to his mother, *"Women, behold, your son!"* 27. Then he said to the disciple, *"Behold, your mother!"* And from that hour the disciple took her to his own home.

28. After this Jesus, knowing that all was now finished, said (to fulfill the scripture), *"I thirst."* 29. A bowl full of vinegar stood there; so they put a sponge full of the vinegar on hyssop and held it to this mouth. 30. When Jesus had received the vinegar, he said, *"It is finished;"* and he bowed his head and gave up his spirit. 31. Since it was the day of Preparation, in order to prevent the bodies from remaining on the cross on the Sabbath (for that Sabbath was a high day), the Jews asked Pilate that their legs might be broken, and that they might be taken away. 32. So the soldiers came and broke the legs of the first, and of the other who had been crucified with him; 33. but when they came to Jesus and saw that he was already dead, they did not break his legs. 34. But one of the soldiers pierced his

side with a spear, and at once there came out blood and water. 35. He who saw it has born witness-his testimony is true, and he knows that he tells the truth-that you also may believe. 36. For these things took place that the scripture might be fulfilled, "Not a bone of him shall be broken." 37. And again another scripture says, "They shall look on him whom they have pierced."

Gospel of St. John 20:19-31   *19. On the evening of that day, the* first day of the week, the doors being shut where the disciples were for fear of the Jews, Jesus came and stood among them and said to them. *"Peace be with you."* 20. When he had said this, he showed them his hands and his side. Then the disciples were glad when they saw the Lord. 21. Jesus said to them again, *"Peace be with you. As the Father has sent me, even so I send you."* 22. And when he had said this, he breathed on them, and said to them, *"Receive the Holy Spirit. 23. If you forgive the sins of any, they are forgiven; if you retain the sins of any, they are retained."*

24. Now Thomas, one of the twelve, called the Twin, was not with them when Jesus came. 25. So the other disciples told him, "We have seen the Lord." But he said to them, "Unless I see in his hands the print of the nails, and place my finger in the mark of the nails, and place my hand in his side, I will not believe."

26. Eight days later, his disciples were again in the house, and Thomas was with them. The doors were shut, but Jesus came and stood among them, and said, *"Peace be with you."* 27. Then he said to Thomas, *"Put your finger here, and see my hands; and put out your hand, and place it in my side; do not be faithless, but*

believing." 28. Thomas answered him, "My Lord and my God!" 29. Jesus said to him, *"Have you believed because you have seen me? Blessed are those who have not seen and yet believe."*

30. Now Jesus did many other signs in the presence of the disciples, which are not written in this book; 31. but these are written that you may believe that Jesus is the Christ, the Son of God, and that believing you may have life in his name.

True Devotion

With Mary

#260. We must do everything with Mary, that is to say, in all our actions we must look upon Mary, although a simple human being, as the perfect model of every virtue and perfection, fashioned by the Holy Spirit for us to imitate, as far as our limited capacity allows. In every action then we should consider how Mary performed it or how she would perform it if she were in our place. For this reason, we must examine and meditate on the great virtues she practiced during her life, especially:

1) Her lively faith, by which she believed the angel's word without the least hesitation, and believed faithfully and constantly even to the foot of the Cross on Calvary.

2) Her deep humility, which made her prefer seclusion, maintain silence, submit to every eventuality and put herself in the last place.

3) Her truly divine purity, which never had and never will have its equal on this side of heaven. And so on for her other virtues.

Remember what I told you before, that Mary is the great, unique mold of God, designed to make living images of God at little cost and in a short time. Anyone who finds this mold and casts himself into it, is soon transformed into our Lord because it is the true likeness of him.

In Mary

#261. We must do everything in Mary. To understand this we must realize that the Blessed Virgin is the true earthly paradise of the new Adam and the ancient paradise was only a symbol of her. (The whole of this number is a commentary on Gen. 2:8-10, on the earthly paradise.) There are in this earthly paradise untold riches, beauties, rarities and delights, which the new Adam, Jesus Christ, has left there. It is in this paradise that he took his delights for nine months, worked his wonders and displayed his riches with the magnificence of God himself. This most holy place consists of only virgin and immaculate soil from which the new Adam was formed with neither spot nor stain by the operation of the Holy Spirit who dwells there. In this earthly paradise grows the real Tree of Life which bore our Lord, the fruit of Life, and the Tree of knowledge of good and evil, which bore the Light of the world.

In this divine place there are trees planted by the hand of God and watered by his divine unction which have borne and continue to bear fruit that is pleasing to him. There are flowers of virtue, diffusing a fragrance which delights even the angels. Here there are meadows verdant with hope, impregnable towers of fortitude, enchanting mansions of confidence, and many other delights.

Only the Holy Spirit can teach us the truths that these material objects symbolize. In this place the air is perfectly pure. There is no night, but only the brilliant day of the sacred humanity, the resplendent, spotless sun of the Divinity, the blazing furnace of love, melting all the base metal thrown into it and changing it into gold. There the river of humility gushes forth the whole of this enchanted place. These branches are the four cardinal virtues.

#262. The Holy Spirit speaking through the Fathers of the Church, also calls our Lady the Eastern Gate, through which the High Priest, Jesus Christ, enters and goes out into the world. (Ezek. 44:1-3) Through this gate he entered the world the first time and through this same gate he will come the second time.

The Holy Spirit also calls her the Sanctuary of the Divinity, the Resting-place of the Holy Trinity, the Throne of God, the City of God, the Altar of God, the Temple of God, the World of God. All these titles and expressions of praise are very real when related to the different wonders the Almighty worked in her and the graces which he bestowed on her. What wealth and what glory! What a joy and a privilege for us to enter and dwell in Mary, in whom almighty God has set up the throne of his supreme glory!

#263. But how difficult it is for us sinners to have the freedom, the ability and the light to enter such an exalted and holy place. This place is guarded not by a cherub, like the first earthly

paradise, but by the Holy Spirit himself who has become its absolute Master. Referring to her, he says, "You are an enclosed garden, my bride, an enclosed garden and a sealed fountain." (Song of Songs 4:12) Mary is enclosed. Mary is sealed. The unfortunate children of Adam and Eve, driven from the earthly paradise, can enter this new paradise only by a special grace of the Holy Spirit which they have to merit.

#264. When we have obtained this remarkable grace by our fidelity, we should be delighted to remain in Mary. We should rest there peacefully, rely on her confidently, hide ourselves there with safety, and abandon ourselves unconditionally to her, so that within her virginal bosom:

1) We may be nourished with the mild of her grace and her motherly compassion.

2) We may be delivered from all anxiety, fear and scruples.

3) We may be safeguarded from all our enemies, the devil, the world and sin which have never gained admittance there. That is why our Lady says that those who work in her will not sin, that is, those who dwell spiritually in our Lady will never commit serious sin.

4) We may be formed in our Lord and our Lord formed in us, because her womb is, as the early Fathers call it, the house of the divine secrets where Jesus and all the elect have been conceived. "This one and that one were born in her."

For Mary

#265. Finally we must do everything for Mary. Since we have given ourselves completely to her service, it is only right that we should do everything for her as if we were her personal servant and slave. This does not mean that we take her for the ultimate end of our service, for Jesus alone is our ultimate end. But we take Mary for our proximate end, our mysterious intermediary and the easiest way of reaching him.

Like every good servant and slave we must not remain idle, but, relying on her protection, we should undertake and carry out great things for our noble Queen. We must defend her privileges when they are questioned and uphold her good name when it is under attack. We must attract everyone, if possible, to her service and to this true and sound devotion. We must speak up and denounce those who distort devotion to her by outraging her Son, and at the same time we must apply ourselves to spreading this true devotion. As a reward for these little services, we should expect nothing in return save the honor of belonging to such a lovable Queen and the joy of being united through her to Jesus, her Son, by a bond that is indissoluble in time and in eternity.

Glory to Jesus in Mary!
Glory to Mary in Jesus!
Glory to God alone!

*"What Jesus meant when he said,
'Behold your Mother' was this:
My wounds are sources of graces which flow only through Mary."*

St. Andrea

How to Make Your Consecration

"At the end of the three weeks," says St. Louis De Montfort, "they shall go to confession and to Communion, with the intention of giving themselves to Jesus Christ in the quality of slaves of love, by the hands of Mary. After Communion, which they should try to make according to the method given further on, they should recite the formula of their consecration, which they will also find further on. They ought to write it, or have it written, unless they have a printed copy of it; and they should sign it the same day they have made it. It would be well also that on that day they should pay some tribute to Jesus Christ and our Blessed Lady, either as a penance for their past unfaithfulness to the vows of their Baptism or as a testimony of their dependence on the dominion of Jesus and Mary. This tribute ought to be according to the devotion and ability of everyone; such as, a fast, a mortification, an alms or a candle. If they had but a pin to give in homage, yet gave it with good heart, it would be enough for Jesus, Who looks only at one's good will. Once a year at least, on the same day, they should renew the same consecration, observing the same practices during the three weeks. They might also once a month, or even once a day, renew all they have done in these few words: "I am all Thine and all that I have belongs to Thee, O my sweet Jesus, through Mary, Thy holy Mother."

For formula of Consecration, see p. 209.

Note from the author - Marian spirituality and devotion, like all authentic devotions, have their foundations in Sacred Scripture,

Sacred Tradition and have been taught by the Magisterium of the Catholic Church. Below you will find a divinely inspired interpretation of the biblical foundations of *True Devotion to the Blessed Mother* that only a saint can so beautifully expound upon. In St. Louis De Montfort's explanation, you will come to understand that true devotion to the Blessed Mother is **not an option**, but a must for all of God's children in order to attain to the fullness of Christ Jesus.

"Always be prepared to make a defense to any one who calls you to account for the hope that is in you."
1 Peter 3:15

THE BIBLICAL FOUNDATION OF TRUE DEVOTION TO JESUS THROUGH MARY CAN BE FOUND IN #'S 183-200

True Devotion

BIBLICAL FIGURE OF THIS PERFECT DEVOTION: REBECCA AND JACOB

#183. The Holy Spirit gives us in Sacred Scripture a striking allegorical figure of all the truths I have been explaining concerning the Blessed Virgin and her children and servants. It is the story of Jacob who received the blessing of his father Isaac through the care and ingenuity of his mother Rebecca.

Here is the story as the Holy Spirit tells it. I shall expound it further later on.

The Story of Jacob (Found in Genesis 25 - 27)

#184. Several years after Esau had sold his birthright to Jacob, Rebecca, their mother, who loved Jacob tenderly, secured this blessing for him by a holy stratagem full of mystery for us.

Isaac, realizing that he was getting old, wished to bless his children before he died. He summoned Esau, who was his favorite son, and told him to go our hunting and bring him something to eat, in order that he might then give him his blessing. Rebecca immediately told Jacob what was happening and sent him to fetch two small goats from the flock. When Jacob gave them to his mother, she cooked them in the way Isaac liked them. Then she dressed Jacob in Esau's clothes which she had in her keeping, and covered his hands and neck with the goat-skin. The father, who was blind, although hearing the voice of Jacob, would think that it was Esau when he touched the skin on his hands.

Isaac was of course surprised at the voice which he thought was Jacob's and told him to come closer. Isaac felt the hair on the skin covering Jacob's hands and said that the voice was indeed like Jacob's but the hands were Esau's. After he had eaten, Isaac kissed Jacob and smelt the fragrance of his scented clothes. He blessed him and called down on him the dew of heaven and the fruitfulness of earth. He made him master of all his brothers and concluded his blessing with these words, "Cursed be those who curse you and blessed be those who bless you."

Isaac had scarcely finished speaking when Esau came in, bringing what he had caught while out hunting. He wanted his father to bless him after he had eaten. The holy patriarch was shocked when he realized what had happened. But far from retracting what he had done, he confirmed it because he clearly saw the finger of God in it all. Then as Holy Scripture relates, Esau began to protest loudly against the treachery of his brother. He then asked his father if he had only one blessing to give. In so doing, as the early Fathers point out, Esau was the symbol of those who are too ready to imagine that there is an alliance between God and the world, because they themselves are eager to enjoy at one and the same time, the blessings of heaven and the blessings of the earth. Isaac was touched by Esau's cries and finally blessed him but only with a blessing of the earth, and he subjected him to his brother. Because of this, Esau conceived such a venomous hatred for Jacob that he could hardly wait for his father's death to kill him. And Jacob would not have escaped death if his dear mother Rebecca had not saved him by her ingenuity and her good advise.

Interpretation of the story

#185. Before explaining this beautiful story, let me remind you that, according to the early Fathers and the interpreters of Holy Scripture, Jacob is the type of our Lord and of souls who are saved, and Esau is the type of souls who are condemned. We have only to examine the actions and conduct of both in order to judge each one.

Within St. Louis De Montfort's interpretation of this biblical event of Rebecca and Jacob, the author has inserted in bold type where each of the *Four Senses* of Sacred Scripture are found. For more understanding on what the Catholic Church teaches about these *Four Senses,* and how we are to adhere to them when interpretating Sacred Scripture, please refer to the *Catechism of the Catholic Church #'s 115-119.*

Literal Sense of Esau
1. Esau, the elder brother, was strong and robust, clever, and skillful with the bow and very successful at hunting.
2. He seldom stayed at home and, relying only on his own

strength and skill, worked out of doors.

3. He never went out of his way to please his mother Rebecca, and did little or nothing for her.
4. He was such a glutton and so fond of eating that he sold his birthright for a dish of lentils.
5. Like Cain, he was extremely jealous of his brother and persecuted him relentlessly.

Allegorical/Typological Sense of Esau-conduct of sinners

#186. This is the usual conduct of sinners:

1) They rely upon their own strength and skill in temporal affairs. They are very energetic, clever and well-informed about things of this world but very dull and ignorant about things of heaven.

Moral Sense of Esau

#187. 2) And so they are never or very seldom at home, in their own house, that is, in their own interior, the inner, essential abode that God has given to every man to dwell in, after his own example, for God always abides within himself. Sinners have no liking for solitude or the spiritual life or interior devotion. They consider those who live an interior life, secluded from the world, and who work more interiorly than exteriorly, as narrow-minded, bigoted and uncivilized.

#188. 3) Sinners care little or nothing about devotion to Mary the Mother of the elect. It is true that they do not really hate her. Indeed they even speak well of her sometimes. They say they love

her and they practice some devotion in her honor. Nevertheless they cannot bear to see anyone love her tenderly, for they do not have for her any of the affection of Jacob; they find fault with the honor which her good children and servants faithfully pay her to win her affection. They think this kind of devotion is not necessary for salvation, and as long as they do not go as far as hating her or openly ridiculing devotion to her they believe they have done all they need to win her good graces. Because they recite or mumble a few prayers to her without any affection and without even thinking of amending their lives, they consider they are our Lady's servants.

Anagogical Sense of Esau

#189. 4) Sinners sell their birthright, that is, the joys of paradise, for a dish of lentils, that is, the pleasures of this world. They laugh, they drink, they eat, they have a good time, they gamble, they dance and so forth, without taking any more trouble than Esau to make themselves worthy of their heavenly Father's blessing. Briefly, they think only of this world, love only the world, speak and act only for the world and its pleasures. For a passing moment of pleasure, for a fleeting wisp of honor, for a piece of hard earth, yellow or white, they barter away their baptismal grace, their robe of innocence and their heavenly inheritance.

#190. 5) Finally, sinners continually hate and persecute the elect, openly or secretly. The elect are a burden to them. They despise them, criticize them, ridicule them, insult them, rob them, deceive them, impoverish them, hunt them down and trample them into the dust; while they themselves are making fortunes, enjoying

themselves, getting good positions for themselves, enriching themselves, rising to power and living in comfort.

Literal Sense of Jacob-type of Jesus and God's chosen ones.

#191. 1) Jacob, the younger son, was of a frail constitution, gentle and peaceable, and usually stayed at home to please his mother, whom he loved so much. If he did go out it was not through any personal desire of his, nor from any confidence in his own ability, but simply out of obedience to his mother.

#192. 2) He loved and honored his mother. That is why he remained at home close to her. He was never happier than when he was in her presence. He avoided everything that might displease her, and did everything he thought would please her. This made Rebecca love him all the more.

#193. 3) He was submissive to his mother in all things. He obeyed her entirely in everything, promptly without delay and lovingly without complaint. At the least indication of her will, young Jacob hastened to comply with it. He accepted whatever she told him without questioning. For instance, when she told him to get two small goats and bring them to her so that she might prepare something for his father Isaac to eat, Jacob did not reply that one would be enough for one man, but without arguing he did exactly what she told him to do.

#194. 4) He had the utmost confidence in his mother. He did not rely on his own ability; he relied solely on his mother's care and protection. He went to her in all his needs and consulted her in all his doubts. For instance, when he asked her if his father, instead of

blessing him, would curse him, he believed her and trusted her when she said she would take the curse upon herself.

#195. 5) Finally, he adopted, as much as he could, the virtues he saw in his mother. It seems that one of the reasons why he spent so much time at home was to imitate his dear mother, who was so virtuous, and to keep away from evil companions, who might lead him into sin. In this way, he made himself worthy to receive the double blessing of his beloved father.

Allegorical/Typological Sense of Jacob and Rebecca – is a type of the Blessed Mother.

#196. It is in a similar manner that God's chosen ones usually act.

Moral Sense of Jacob

1) They stay at home with their mother – that is, they have an esteem for quietness, love the interior life and are assiduous in prayer. They always remain in the company of the Blessed Virgin, their Mother and Model, whose glory is wholly interior and who during her whole life dearly loved seclusion and prayer. It is true, at times they do venture out into the world, but only to fulfill the duties of their state of life, in obedience to the will of God and the will of their Mother.

No matter how great their accomplishments may appear to others, they attach far more importance to what they do within themselves in their interior life, in the company of the Blessed Virgin. For there they work at the great task of perfection, compared to which all other work is mere child's play. At times their brothers and sisters are working outside with great energy, skill and success, and win the praise and approbation of the world. But they know by the light of the Holy Spirit, that there is far more good, more glory and more joy in remaining hidden and recollected with our Lord, in complete and perfect submission to Mary, than there is in performing by themselves marvelous works of nature and grace in the world like so many Esaus and sinners. Glory for God and riches for men are in her house. (Ps. 111:3)

Lord Jesus, how lovely is your dwelling place! The sparrow has found a home to dwell in, and the turtle-dove a nest for her little ones! (Ps. 83:4) How happy is the man who dwells in the house of Mary, where you were the first to dwell! Here in this home of the elect, he draws from you alone the help he needs to climb the stairway of virtue he has built in his heart to the highest possible point of perfection while in this vale of tears.

#197. 2) The elect have a great love for our Lady and honor her truly as their Mother and Queen. They love her not merely in word but in deed. They honor her not just outwardly, but from the depths of their heart. Like Jacob, they avoid the least thing that might displease her, and eagerly do whatever they think might win her favor. As Jacob brought Rebecca two young goats, they bring Mary their body and their soul, with all their faculties,

- a) that she may accept them as her own;
- b) that she may make them die to sin and self by divesting them of self-love, in order to please Jesus her Son, who wishes to have as friends and disciples only those who are dead to sin and self,
- c) that she may clothe them according to their heavenly

Father's taste and for his greater glory, which she knows better than any other creature,

d) that through her care and intercession, this body and soul of theirs, thoroughly cleansed from every stain, thoroughly dead to self, thoroughly stripped and well-prepared, may be pleasing to the heavenly Father and deserving of his blessing.

Is this not what those chosen souls do who, to prove to Jesus and Mary how effective and courageous is their love, live and esteem the perfect consecration to Jesus through Mary which we are now teaching them?

Sinners may say that they love Jesus, that they love and honor Mary, but they do not do so with their whole heart and soul. Unlike the elect, they do not love Jesus and Mary enough to consecrate to them their body with its senses and their soul with its passions.

According to St. Louis De Montfort, the Historical Event of the Account of Rebecca and Jacob is a Prefigurement of the Wedding Feast at Cana (John 2:1-25).

#198. 3) They are subject and obedient to our Lady, their good Mother, and here they are simply following the example set by our Lord himself, who spent thirty of the thirty-three years he lived on earth glorifying God his Father in perfect and entire submission to his holy Mother. They obey her, following her advice to the letter, just as Jacob followed that of Rebecca, when she said to him, *"My son, follow my advice";* or like the stewards at the wedding in Cana,

to whom our Lady said, *"Do whatever he tells you."*

Through obedience to his Mother, Jacob received the blessing almost by a miracle, because in the natural course of events he should not have received it. As a reward for following the advice of our Lady, the stewards at the wedding in Cana were honored with the first of our Lord's miracles when, at her request he changed water into wine. In the same way, until the end of time, all who are to receive the blessing of our heavenly Father and who are to be honored with his wondrous graces will receive them only as a result of their perfect obedience to Mary. On the other hand the "Esaus" will lose their blessings because of their lack of submission to the Blessed Virgin.

#199. 4) They have great confidence in the goodness and power of the Blessed Virgin, their dear Mother, and incessantly implore her help. They take her for their pole-star to lead them safely into harbor. They open their hearts to her and tell her their troubles and their needs. They rely on her mercy and kindness to obtain forgiveness for their sins through her intercession and to experience her motherly comfort in their troubles and anxieties. They even cast themselves into her virginal bosom, hide and lose themselves there in a wonderful manner. There they are filled with pure love, they are purified from the least stain of sin, and they find Jesus in all his fullness. For he reigns in Mary as if on the most glorious of thrones. What incomparable happiness! Abbot Guerric says, "Do not imagine there is more joy in dwelling in Abraham's bosom than in Mary's, for it is in her that our Lord placed his throne."

Sinners, on the other hand, put all their confidence in

themselves. Like the prodigal son, they eat with the swine. Like toads they feed on earth. Like all worldlings, they love only visible and external things. They do not know the sweetness of Mary's bosom. They do not have that reliance and confidence which the elect have for the Blessed Virgin, their Mother. Deplorably they choose to satisfy their hunger elsewhere, as St. Gregory says, because they do not want to taste the sweetness already prepared within themselves and within Jesus and Mary

Anagogical Sense of Jacob - Prefiguring those who have true devotion to the Blessed Mother and Esau – those who do not have a true devotion to the Blessed Mother.

#200. 5) Finally, chosen souls keep to the ways of the Blessed Virgin, their loving Mother – that is, they imitate her and so are sincerely happy and devout and bear the infallible sign of God's chosen ones. This loving Mother says to them, "Happy are those who keep my ways," (Prov. 8:32) which means, happy are those who practice my virtues and who, with the help of God's grace, follow the path of my life. They are happy in this world because of the abundance of grace and sweetness I impart to them out of my fullness, and which they receive more abundantly than others who do not imitate me so closely. They are happy at the hour of death which is sweet and peaceful for I am usually there myself to lead them home to everlasting joy. Finally, they will be happy for all eternity, because no servant of mine who imitated my virtues during life has ever been lost.

On the other hand, sinners are unhappy during their life, at their death, and throughout eternity, because they do not imitate the virtues of our Lady. They are satisfied with going no further than joining her confraternities, reciting a few prayers in her honor, or performing other exterior devotional exercises.

O Blessed Virgin, my dear Mother, how happy are those who faithfully keep your ways, your counsels, and your commands; who never allow themselves to be led astray by a false devotion to you! But how unhappy and accursed are those who abuse devotion to you by not keeping the commandments of your Son. *"They are accursed who stray from your commandments." (Ps. 118:21)*

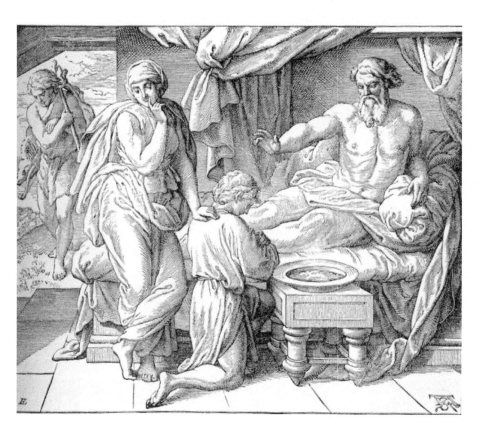

PRAYERS

Veni Creator

Come, O Creator Spirit blest!
And in our souls take up Thy rest;
Come with Thy grace and heavenly aid,
To fill the hearts which Thou hast made.

Great Paraclete! To Thee we cry,
O highest gift of God most high!
O font of life! O fire of love!
And sweet anointing from above.

Thou in Thy sevenfold gifts art known,
The finger of God's hand we own;
The promise of the Father, Thou!
Who dost the tongue with power endow.

Kindle our senses from above,
And make our hearts o'erflow with love;
With patience firm and virtue high
The weakness of our flesh supply.

Far from us drive the foe we dread,
And grant us Thy true peace instead;
So shall we not, with Thee for guide,
Turn from the path of life aside.

Oh, may Thy grace on us bestow
The Father and the Son to know,
And Thee, through endless times confessed,
Of both, the eternal Spirit blest.

All glory while the ages run
Be to the Father and the Son
Who rose from death; the same to Thee,
O Holy Ghost, eternally. Amen.

Ave Maris Stella

Hail, bright Star of Ocean,
God's own Mother blest,
Ever sinless Virgin,
Gate of heavenly rest.

Taking that sweet Ave
Which from Gabriel came,
Peace confirm within us,
Changing Eva's name.

Break the captives' fetters,
Light on blindness pour,
All our ills expelling,
Every bliss implore.

Show thyself a Mother;
May the Word Divine,
Born for us thy Infant,
Hear our prayers through thine.

Virgin all excelling,
Mildest of the mild,
Freed from guilt, preserve us,
Pure and undefiled.

Keep our life all spotless,
Make our way secure,
Till we find in Jesus
Joy forevermore.

Through the highest Heaven
To the Almighty Three,
Father, Son and Spirit,
One same glory be. Amen.

Magnificat

My soul doth magnify the Lord. And my spirit hath rejoiced in God my Saviour. Because He hath regarded the humility of His handmaid; for behold, from henceforth all generation shall call me blessed. Because He that is mighty hath done great things to me; and holy is His name. And His mercy is from generation unto generation, on those who fear Him. He hath shown might in His arm; He hath scattered the proud in the conceit of their heart. Put down the mighty from their thrones; and exalted the humble. He hath filled the hungry with good things; and the rich He hath sent empty away. He hath received Israel His servant, being mindful of His mercy. As He spoke to our Fathers, to Abraham and to his seed forever. Glory be to the Father and to the Son and to the Holy Ghost as it was in the beginning is now and ever shall be world without end. Amen.

Prayer to Mary
By Saint Louis Marie De Montfort

Hail Mary, beloved Daughter of the Eternal Father! Hail Mary, admirable Mother of the Son! Hail Mary, faithful Spouse of the Holy Ghost! Hail Mary, my dear Mother, my loving Mistress, my powerful Sovereign! Hail my joy, my glory, my heart and my soul! Thou art all mine by mercy, and I am all thine by justice. But I am not yet sufficiently thine. I now give myself wholly to thee without keeping anything back for myself or others. If thou still seest in me anything which does not belong to thee, I beseech thee to take it and to make thyself the absolute Mistress of all that is mine. Destroy in me all that may be displeasing to God, root it up and bring it to naught; place and cultivate in me everything that is pleasing to thee.

May the light of thy faith dispel the darkness of my mind; may thy profound humility take the place of my pride; may thy sublime contemplation check the distractions of my wondering imagination; may thy continuous sight of God fill my memory with His presence; may the burning love of thy heart inflame the lukewarmness of mine; may thy virgin take the place of my sins; may thy merits be my only adornment in the sight of God and make up for all that is wanting in me. Finally, dearly beloved Mother, grant, if it be possible, that I may have no other heart but thine to praise and glorify the Lord; that I may have no other heart but thine to love God with a love as pure and ardent as thine. I do not ask thee for visions, revelations, sensible devotion or spiritual pleasures. It is thy privilege to see God clearly; it is thy privilege to enjoy heavenly bliss; it is thy privilege to triumph gloriously in Heaven at the right hand of thy Son and to hold absolute sway over angels, men and demons; it is thy privilege to dispose of all gifts of God, just as thou willest.

Such is, O heavenly Mary, the "best part," which the Lord has given thee and which shall never be taken away from thee,-and this thought fills my heart with joy. As for my part here below, I wish for no other than that which was thine: To believe sincerely without spiritual pleasures; to suffer joyfully without human consolation; to die continually to myself without respite; and to work zealously and unselfishly for thee until death as the humblest of thy servants. The only grace I beg thee to obtain for me is that every day and every moment of my life I may say: Amen, so be it-to all that thou didst do while on earth; Amen, so be it-to all that thou art now doing in Heaven; Amen, so be it-to all that thou art doing in my soul, so that thou alone mayest fully glorify Jesus in me for time and eternity. Amen.

Saint Augustine's Prayer

Thou art Christ, my holy Father, my tender God, my great King, my good Shepherd, my one Master, my best Helper, my most Beautiful and my Beloved, my living Bread, my Priest forever, my Leader to my country, my true Light, my holy Sweetness, my straight Way, my excellent Wisdom, my pure Simplicity, my pacific Harmony, my whole Guard, my good Portion, my everlasting Salvation.

Christ Jesus, my sweet Lord, why have I ever loved, why in my whole life have I ever desired anything except Thee, Jesus my God? Where was I when I was not in Thy mind with Thee? Now, from this time forth, do you, all my desires, grow hot, and flow out upon the Lord Jesus; run, you have been tardy thus far; hasten whither you are going; seek Whom you are seeking. O Jesus, may he who loves Thee not, be anathema; may he who loves Thee not, be filled with bitterness!

O sweet Jesus, may every good feeling that is fitted for Thy praise, love Thee, delight in Thee, admire Thee. God of my heart and my Portion, Christ Jesus, may my heart faint away in spirit and mayest Thou be my life within me! May the live coal of Thy love grow hot within my spirit, and break forth into a perfect fire; may it burn incessantly on the altar of my heart; may it glow in my innermost being; may it blaze in hidden recesses of my soul; and in the day of my consummation, may I be found consummated with Thee. Amen

Prayer to Jesus
By Saint Louis Marie De Montfort

O most loving Jesus, deign to let me pour forth my gratitude before Thee, for the grace Thou hast bestowed upon me in giving me to Thy holy Mother through the devotion of Holy Bondage, that she may be my advocate in the presence of Thy majesty and my support in my extreme misery. Alas, O Lord! I am so wretched that without this dear Mother I should be certainly lost. Yes, Mary is necessary for me at Thy side and everywhere: that she may appease Thy just wrath, because I have so often offended Thee; that she may save me from the eternal punishment of Thy justice, which I deserve; that she may contemplate Thee, speak to Thee, pray to Thee, approach Thee and please Thee; that she may help me to save my soul and the souls of others; in short, Mary is necessary for me that I may always do Thy holy will and seek Thy greater glory in all things. Ah, would that I could proclaim throughout the whole world the mercy that Thou hast shown to me! Would that everyone might know I should be already damned, were it not for Mary! Would that I might offer worthy thanksgiving for so great a blessing! Mary is in me. Oh, what a treasure! Oh, what a consolation! And shall I not be entirely hers? Oh, what ingratitude! My dear Saviour, send me death rather than such a calamity, for I would rather die than live without belonging entirely to Mary. With Saint John the Evangelist at the foot of the Cross, I have taken her a thousand times for my own and as many times have given myself to her; but if I have not yet done it as Thou, dear Jesus, dost wish, I now renew this offering as Thou dost desire me to renew it. And if Thou see in my soul or my body anything that does not belong to this august princess, I pray Thee to take it and cast it far from me, for whatever in me does not belong to Mary is unworthy of Thee.

O Holy Spirit, grant me all these graces. Plant in my soul the Tree of true Life, which is Mary; cultivate it and tend it so that it may grow and blossom and bring forth the fruit of life in abundance. O Holy Spirit, give me great devotion to Mary, Thy faithful Spouse; give me great confidence in her maternal heart and an abiding refuge in her mercy, so that by her Thou may truly form in me Jesus Christ, great and mighty, unto the fullness of His perfect age. Amen

O Jesus Living in Mary

O Jesus living in Mary,

Come and live in Thy servants,

In the spirit of Thy holiness,

In the fullness of Thy might,

In the truth of Thy virtues,

In the perfection of Thy ways,

In the communion of Thy mysteries;

Subdue every hostile power

In Thy spirit, for the glory of the Father. Amen.

Sub Tuum Praesidium

We fly to thy patronage, O holy Mother of God; despise not thou our petitions in our necessities, but deliver us from all danger, O ever glorious and blessed Virgin.

Memorare

Remember, O most gracious Virgin Mary, that never was it known that anyone who fled to thy protection, implored thy help, or sought thy intercession, was left unaided. Filled, therefore, with confidence, I fly unto thee, O Virgin of Virgins, my Mother! To thee I come, before thee I stand, sinful and sorrowful. O Mother of the Word Incarnate! Despise not my petitions, but in thy mercy, hear and answer me. Amen.

Litanies

Litany of the Holy Ghost

Lord, have mercy on us.
Christ, have mercy on us.
Lord, have mercy on us.
Father all powerful, *have mercy on us.*
Jesus, Eternal son of the Father, Redeemer of the world, *save us.*
Holy Trinity, *hear us.*

Holy Ghost, Who proceeds from the Father and the Son, *enter our hearts.*
Holy Ghost, Who art equal to the Father and the Son, *enter our hearts.*

Promise of God the Father, *Have mercy on us.*
Ray of heavenly light,
Author of all good,
Source of heavenly water,
Consuming fire,
Ardent charity,
Spiritual unction,
Spirit of love and truth,
Spirit of wisdom and understanding,
Spirit of counsel and fortitude,
Spirit of knowledge and piety,

Spirit of the fear of the Lord,

Spirit of grace and prayer,

Spirit of peace and meekness,

Spirit of modesty and innocence,

Holy Ghost, the Comforter,

Holy Ghost, the Sanctifier,

Holy Ghost who governs the Church,

Gift of God, the Most High,

Spirit Who fills the universe,

Spirit of the adoption of the children of God, ⇧

Holy Ghost, *inspire us with the horror of sin.*

Holy Ghost, *come and renew the face of the earth.*

Holy Ghost, *shed Thy light in our souls.*

Holy Ghost, *engrave Thy law in our hearts.*

Holy Ghost, *inflame us with the flame of Thy love.*

Holy Ghost, *open to us the treasures of Thy graces.*

Holy Ghost, *teach us to pray well.*

Holy Ghost, *enlighten us with Thy heavenly inspirations.*

Holy Ghost, *lead us in the way of salvation.*

Holy Ghost, *grant us the only necessary knowledge.*

Holy Ghost, *inspire in us the practice of good.*

Holy Ghost, *grant us the merits of all virtues.*

Holy Ghost, *make us preserve in justice.*

Holy Ghost, *be Thou our everlasting reward.*

Lamb of God, Who takes away the sins of the world, *Send us Thy Holy Ghost.*

Lamb of God, Who takes away the sins of the world, *Pour down into our* souls *the gifts of the Holy Ghost.*

Lamb of God, Who takes away the sins of the world, *Grant us the Spirit of wisdom and piety.*

    IV.   Come, Holy Ghost! Fill the hearts of Thy faithful.

    R.   *And enkindle in them the fire of Thy love.*

Let us pray

    Grant, O merciful Father, that Thy Divine Spirit may enlighten, inflame and purify us, that He may penetrate us with His heavenly dew and make us fruitful in good works, through our Lord Jesus Christ, Thy Son, Who with Thee, in the unity of the same Spirit, lives and reigns forever and ever. Amen.

Litany of the Blessed Virgin

Lord, have mercy on us.
Christ, have mercy in us.
Lord, have mercy on us. Christ, hear us.
Christ, graciously hear us.

God the Father of Heaven, *have mercy on us.*
God the Son, Redeemer of the world, *have mercy on us.*
God the Holy Ghost, *have mercy on us.*
Holy Mary, *pray for us.*
Holy Mother of God,
Holy Virgin of virgins,
Mother of Christ,

Mother of divine grace,

Mother most pure,

Mother most chaste,

Mother inviolate,

Mother undefiled,

Mother most amiable,

Mother most admirable,

Mother of good counsel,

Mother of our Creator,

Mother of our Savior,

Mother of the Church,

Virgin most prudent,

Virgin most venerable,

Virgin most renowned,

Virgin most powerful,

Virgin most merciful,

Virgin most faithful,

Mirror of justice,

Seat of Wisdom,

Cause of our joy,

Spiritual vessel,

Vessel of honor,

Singular vessel of devotion,

Mystical rose,

Tower of David,

Tower of ivory,

House of gold,

Ark of the covenant,

Gate of Heaven,

Morning star,

Health of the sick,

Refuge of sinners,

Comforter of the afflicted,

Help of Christians,

Queen of angels,

Queen of patriarchs,

Queen of prophets,

Queen of Apostles,

Queen of martyrs,

Queen of confessors,

Queen of virgins,

Queen of all saints,

Queen conceived without Original Sin,

Queen assumed into heaven,

Queen of the most holy Rosary,

Queen of peace,

Lamb of God, Who takes away the sins of the world, *Spare us, O Lord.*

Lamb of God, Who takes away the sins of the world, *Graciously hear us, O Lord.*

Lamb of God, Who takes away the sins of the world, *Have mercy on us.*

V. Pray for us, O holy Mother of God,

R. That we may be made worthy of the promises of Christ.

Let us pray

Grant unto us, Thy servants, we beseech Thee, O Lord God, at all times to enjoy health of soul and body, and by the glorious intercession of Blessed Mary, ever virgin, when freed from the sorrows of this present life, to enter into the joy of Thine eternal gladness. Through Christ our Lord. Amen.

Litany of the Holy Name of Jesus

Lord, have mercy on us.
Christ, have mercy on us.
Lord, have mercy on us. Jesus, hear us.
Jesus, graciously hear us.

God the Father of Heaven, *Have mercy on us.*
God the Son, Redeemer of the world,
God the Holy Ghost,
Holy Trinity, One God,
Jesus, Son of the living God,
Jesus, splendor of the Father,
Jesus, brightness of eternal light,
Jesus, King of glory,
Jesus, sun of justice,
Jesus, Son of the Virgin Mary,
Jesus, most amiable,
Jesus, most admirable,

Jesus, mighty God,

Jesus, Father of the world to come,

Jesus, angel of great counsel,

Jesus, most powerful,

Jesus, most patient,

Jesus, most obedient,

Jesus, meek and humble of heart,

Jesus, lover of chastity,

Jesus, lover of us,

Jesus, God of peace,

Jesus, author of life,

Jesus, model of virgins,

Jesus, lover of souls,

Jesus, our God,

Jesus, our refuge,

Jesus, Father of the poor,

Jesus, treasure of the faithful,

Jesus, Good Shepherd,

Jesus, true light,

Jesus, eternal wisdom,

Jesus, infinite goodness,

Jesus, our way and our life,

Jesus, joy of angels,

Jesus, King of patriarchs,

Jesus, master of Apostles,

Jesus, teacher of Evangelists,

Jesus, strength of martyrs,

Jesus, light of confessors,

Jesus, purity of virgins,

Jesus, crown of all saints,

Be merciful, *spare us, O Jesus.*

Be merciful, *graciously hear us, O Jesus.*

From all evil, *Jesus, deliver us.*

From all sin,

From Thy wrath,

From the snares of the Devil,

From the spirit of fornication,

From everlasting death,

From the neglect of Thine inspirations,

Through the mystery of Thy holy Incarnation,

Through Thy nativity,

Through Thine infancy,

Through Thy most divine life,

Through Thy labors,

Through Thine agony and Passion,

Through Thy cross and dereliction,

Through Thy sufferings,

Through Thy death and burial,

Through Thy Resurrection,

Through Thine Ascension,

Through Thine institution of the most Holy Eucharist,

Through Thy joys,

Through Thy glory, ⇑

Lamb of God, Who takes away the sins of the world, *Spare us, O Lord.*

Lamb of God, Who takes away the sins of the world, *Graciously hear us, O Jesus.*

Lamb of God, Who takes away the sins of the world, *Have mercy on us.*

Jesus, hear us. *Jesus, graciously hear us.*

Let us pray

O Lord Jesus Christ, Who hast said: Ask and you shall receive, seek and you shall find, knock and it shall be opened unto you; grant, we beseech Thee, to us who ask the gift of Thy divine love, that we may ever love Thee with all our hearts, and in all our words and actions, and never cease from praising Thee.

Give us, O Lord, a perpetual fear and love of Thy holy Name; for Thou never failest to govern those whom Thou dost solidly establish in Thy love, Who livest and reignest world without end. Amen

Litany of the Sacred Heart

Lord, have mercy on us.
Christ, have mercy on us.
Lord, have mercy on us. Christ, hear us.
Christ, graciously hear us.

God the Father of Heaven, *have mercy on us.*
God the Son, Redeemer of the world, *have mercy on us.*
God the Holy Ghost, *have mercy on us.*
Holy Trinity, One God, *have mercy on us.*
Heart of Jesus, Son of the Eternal Father, ℣
Heart of Jesus, formed by the Holy Ghost in the womb of the Virgin Mother,
Heart of Jesus, substantially united with the Word of God,
Heart of Jesus, of infinite majesty,
Heart of Jesus, holy temple of God,
Heart of Jesus, tabernacle of the Most High,
Heart of Jesus, house of God and gate of Heaven,
Heart of Jesus, burning furnace of charity,
Heart of Jesus, abode of justice and love,
Heart of Jesus, full of goodness and love,
Heart of Jesus, abyss of all virtues,
Heart of Jesus, most worthy of all praise,
Heart of Jesus, King and center of all hearts,
Heart of Jesus in Whom are all the treasures of wisdom and knowledge,

Heart of Jesus, in Whom dwells all fullness of divinity,

Heart of Jesus, in Whom the Father was well pleased,

Heart of Jesus, of Whose fullness we have all received,

Heart of Jesus, desire of the everlasting hills,

Heart of Jesus, patient and most merciful,

Heart of Jesus, enriching all who invoke Thee,

Heart of Jesus, fountain of life and holiness,

Heart of Jesus, propitiation for our sins,

Heart of Jesus, loaded down with opprobrium,

Heart of Jesus, bruised for our offenses,

Heart of Jesus, obedient unto death,

Heart of Jesus, pierced with a lance,

Heart of Jesus, source of all consolation,

Heart of Jesus, our life and resurrection,

Heart of Jesus, our peace and reconciliation,

Heart of Jesus, victim for sin,

Heart of Jesus, salvation of those who trust in Thee,

Heart of Jesus, hope of those who die in Thee,

Heart of Jesus, delight of all the saints, ⇑

Lamb of God, Who takes away the sins of the world, *Spare us, O Lord.*

Lamb of God, Who takes away the sins of the world, *Graciously hear us, O Lord.*

Lamb of God, Who takes away the sins of the world, *Have mercy on us.*

    V. Jesus meek and humble of heart,

R. Make our hearts like unto Thine.

Let us pray

Almighty and everlasting God, graciously regard the Heart of Thy well beloved Son and the acts of praise and satisfaction which He renders Thee on behalf of sinners; appeased by worthy homage, pardon those who implore Thy mercy, in the name of he same Jesus Christ Thy Son, Who liveth and reigneth with Thee, world without end. Amen.

Renewal of Baptismal Vows

Almighty and eternal God! Thou knowest all things: Thou seest the very bottom of my heart, and Thou knowest that, however sinful I have hitherto been, I am resolved, by the help of Thy grace, to love and serve Thee for the remainder of my life. And therefore, O my God, kneeling before the throne of Thy mercy, I renew, with all sincerity of my soul the promises and vows made for me in my baptism.

I renounce Satan with my whole heart, and will henceforth have no connection with him. I renounce all the pomp's of Satan, that is, all the vanities of the world, the false treasures of its riches, honors and pleasures, and all its corrupt teachings. I renounce all the works of Satan, that is, all kinds of sins.

To Thee alone, O my God, I desire to cling; Thy word will I hear and obey; for Thee alone I desire to live and to die. Amen.

The Act of Consecration

The Act of Consecration to Jesus Christ, the Incarnate Wisdom, through the Blessed Virgin Mary

Eternal and Incarnate Wisdom, most lovable and adorable Jesus, true God and true man, only Son of the eternal Father, and of Mary, always virgin, I adore you profoundly, in dwelling in the splendor of your Father from all eternity and in the virginal womb of Mary, your most worthy Mother, in the time of Your Incarnation.

I thank you for having emptied yourself in assuming the condition of a slave to set me free from the cruel slavery of the evil one.

I praise and glorify you for having willingly chosen to obey Mary, your holy Mother, in all things, so that through her I may be your faithful slave of love.

But I must confess that I have not kept the vows and promises which I made to you so solemnly at my baptism. I have not fulfilled my obligations, and I do not deserve to be called your child or even your loving slave.

Since I cannot lay claim to anything except what merits your rejection and displeasure, I dare no longer approach the holiness of your majesty on my own. That is why I turn to the intercession and the mercy of your holy Mother, whom you yourself have given me to mediate with you. Through her I hope to obtain from you contrition, and pardon for my sins, and that Wisdom whom I desire to dwell in me always.

I turn to you, then, Mary immaculate, living tabernacle of God. The eternal Wisdom, hidden in you, willed to receive the adoration of both men and angels.

I greet you, then, as Queen of heaven and earth. All that is under God has been made subject to your sovereignty.

I call upon you as the unfailing refuge of sinners. In your mercy you have never forsaken anyone.

I, an unfaithful sinner, renew and ratify today through you my baptismal promises. I renounce for ever Satan, his empty promises and his evil designs, and I give myself completely to Jesus Christ, the Incarnate Wisdom, to carry my cross after. him for the rest of my life, and to be more faithful to him that I have been till now.

This day, with the whole court of heaven as witness, I choose you, Mary, as my Mother and Queen. I surrender and consecrate myself to you, body and soul, with all that I possess, both spiritual and material, and even the value of all my actions, past, present and to come. I give you the full right to dispose of me and all that belongs to me, without any reservations, in whatever way you please, for the greater glory of God, in time and throughout eternity.

Accept, gracious Virgin, this little offering of my slavery to honour and imitate that obedience which the eternal Wisdom willingly chose to have towards you, his Mother. I wish to acknowledge the authority which both of you have over this little worm and pitiful sinner. By it I wish to thank God for the privileges bestowed on you by the Blessed Trinity. I solemnly declare that for the future I will try to honor and obey you in all things as your true slave of love.

O admirable Mother, present me to your dear Son as his slave now and for always, so that he who has redeemed me through you, will now receive me through you.

Mother of mercy, grant me the favor of obtaining the true Wisdom of God, and so make me one of those whom you love, teach and guide, whom you nourish and protect as you children and slaves.

Virgin most faithful, make me in everything so committed a disciple, imitator, and slave of Jesus your Son, the Incarnate Wisdom, that I may become, through your intercession and example, fully mature with the fullness which Jesus possessed on earth, and with the fullness of his glory of his in heaven. Amen.

Special Prayers and Practices Concerning the Blessed Virgin Mary

The Fifteen Promises of Mary To Christians Who Recite The Holy Rosary

(Given to St. Dominic and Blessed Alan)

Imprimatur: Patrick J. Hayes, D.D., Archbishop of New York

1. Whoever shall faithfully serve me by the recitation of the rosary, shall receive signal graces.

2. I promise my special protection and the greatest graces to all those who shall recite the rosary.

3. The rosary shall be a powerful armour against hell, it will destroy vice, decrease sin, and defeat heresies.

4. It will cause virtue and good works to flourish; it will obtain for souls the abundant mercy of God; it will withdraw the hearts of men from the love of the world and its vanities, and will lift them to the desire of eternal things. Oh, that souls would sanctify themselves by this means.

5. The soul which recommends itself to me by the recitation of the rosary, shall not perish.

6. Whoever shall recite the rosary devoutly, applying himself to the consideration of its sacred mysteries shall never be conquered by misfortune. God will not chastise him in His justice, he shall not perish by an unprovided death; if he be just he shall remain in the grace of God, and become worthy of eternal life.

7. Whoever shall have a true devotion for the rosary shall not die without the sacraments of the Church.

8. Those who are faithful to recite the rosary shall have during their life and at their death the light of God and the plentitude of His graces; at the moment of death they shall participate in the merits of the saints in paradise.

9. I shall deliver from purgatory those who have been devoted to the rosary.

10. The faithful children of the rosary shall merit a high degree of glory in heaven.

11. You shall obtain all you ask of me by the recitation of the rosary.

12. All those who propagate the holy rosary shall be aided by me in their necessities.

13. I have obtained from my Divine Son that all the advocates of the rosary shall have for intercessors the entire celestial court during their life and at the hour of death.

14. All who recite the rosary are my sons, and brothers of my only son Jesus Christ.

15. Devotion of my rosary is a great sign of predestination.

Mysteries of the Holy Rosary

JOYFUL MYSTERIES

1st Joyful Mystery
The Annunciation
Fruit: Humility

2nd Joyful Mystery
The Visitation
Fruit: Fraternal Charity

3rd Joyful Mystery
Birth of our Lord, Jesus
Fruit: Esteem of spiritual values

4th Joyful Mystery
Presentation in the Temple
Fruit: Purity and Obedience

5th Joyful Mystery
Finding in the Temple
Fruit: Fidelity to one's duties

SORROWFUL MYSTERIES

1st Sorrowful Mystery
Agony of our Lord
Fruit: Sorrow for sin

2nd Sorrowful Mystery
Scourging at the pillar
Fruit: Mortification of senses

3rd Sorrowful Mystery
Crowning with thorns
Fruit: Love of humiliation

4ᵗʰ Sorrowful Mystery
Carrying of the cross
Fruit: Bearing of trials

5ᵗʰ Sorrowful Mystery
Crucifixion
Fruit: Forgiveness of injuries

GLORIOUS MYSTERIES

1ˢᵗ Glorious Mystery
Resurrection
Fruit: Faith and Hope

2ⁿᵈ Glorious Mystery
Ascension
Fruit: Desire of Heaven

3ʳᵈ Glorious Mystery
Descent of the Holy Spirit
Fruit: The Gifts of the Holy Spirit

4ᵗʰ Glorious Mystery
Assumption
Fruit: Devotion to Mary

5ᵗʰ Glorious Mystery
Crowning of Our Blessed Lady
Fruit: Perseverance

LUMINIOUS MYSTERIES

1st Luminous Mystery
Baptism of Jesus in the Jordan
Fruit: Submission to the Will of the Father

2nd Luminous Mystery
The Self-Manifestation at the Wedding of Cana
Fruit: Faith

3rd Luminous Mystery
The Proclamation of the Kingdom with the Call to Conversion
Fruit: Sincere Repentance

4th Luminous Mystery
The Transfiguration
Fruit: Hope

5th Luminous Mystery
The Institution of the Holy Eucharist
Fruit: Intimate Communion with God

The Five First Saturdays

The Promise

On December 10, 1925, Our Lady promised Sister Lucia she would "…assist at the hour of death, with the graces necessary for salvation, all those who on the first Saturdays of five consecutive months confess, receive Holy Communion, pray a Rosary, and keep me company for a quarter of an hour mediating on the fifteen mysteries with the intention of offering me reparation."

How to do the Five First Saturdays

There are four requirements to faithfully fulfill the five first Saturdays.

1. Go to confession.
2. Receive Holy Communion.
3. Say five decades of the Holy Rosary.
4. Mediate for fifteen minutes on the mysteries of the Holy Rosary. (Separate from saying the Rosary.)

During the apparition of February 15, 1926, Sister Lucia presented Our Lord the problem some people had if confessing on Saturdays. She asked Our Lord if the confession would be valid if done within a period of eight days before or eight days after the first Saturday. Our Lord answered: "Yes, it can even be within many more days, provided they are in the state of grace when they receive Me, and have the intention of offering reparation to the Immaculate Heart of Mary."

The Intention

To console the Immaculate Heart of Mary, offer reparation for the blasphemies and ingratitude of unrepentant sinners, and for peace in the world.

The Reasons for this Devotion

On May 29, 1930 Our Lord explained to Sister Lucia why five First Saturdays.

"My daughter, the reason is simple. Against the Immaculate Heart of Mary, five kinds of offenses and blasphemies are committed:

1. Those committed against the Immaculate Conception;
2. Those committed against the virginity of Our Lady;
3. Those committed against the Divine maternity, refusing at the same time, to accept her as the mother of men;

4. Those committed by men who publicly attempt to instill indifference, scorn and even hatred for this Immaculate Mother in the hearts of children;

5. Those committed by men who insult her directly in her statues."

THE SEVEN DOIORS OF MARY

Here are seven graces the Blessed Virgin Mary grants to the souls who honor her daily by saying seven Hail Mary's and meditating on her tears and dolors. This devotion was passed to us by St. Bridget.

1. I will grant peace to their families.
2. They will be enlightened about the divine mysteries.
3. I will console them in their pains and I will accompany them in their work.
4. I will give them as much as they ask for as long as it does not oppose the adorable will of my Divine Son or the sanctification of their souls.
5. I will defend them in their spiritual battles with the infernal enemy and I will protect them at every instant of their lives.
6. I will visible help them at the moment of their death, they will see the face of their Mother.
7. I have obtained (This Grace) from my Divine Son, that those who propagate this devotion to my tears and dolors, will be taken directly from this earthly life to eternal happiness since all their sins will be forgiven and my Son will be their eternal consolation and joy.

The Seven Dolors Of Mary

1. The Prophecy of Simeon.
2. The Flight into Egypt.
3. The Loss of the Child Jesus in the Temple.
4. The Meeting of Jesus and Mary on the Way of the Cross.
5. The Crucifixion.
6. The Taking Down of the Body of Jesus from the Cross.
7. The Burial of Jesus.

Miraculous Medal

In 1830, during the apparitions in the chapel of Rue du Bac in Paris, the Holy Virgin presented the Miraculous Medal to St. Catherine Laboure: Those who wear it, blessed, around their neck will receive great graces. The graces will be abundant for those who wear it with confidence."

At the time of St. Catherine Laboure's death, the distribution of the medal in the world had surpassed the one billion mark. The innumerable conversion, cures and cases of extraordinary protection quickly led to its being called the "Miraculous Medal."

By wearing and disseminating the Miraculous Medal means placing oneself under the protection of the Most Holy Virgin. It means placing oneself under the sign of the Immaculate and taking a stand in the face of the troubles and indifference affecting the modern world.

"The whole world will be overwhelmed by misfortunes of all kinds… All will seem lost, but I shall be with you," the Holy Virgin promised St. Catherine, who repeated this prophesy till the end of her life.

The Blessed Virgin Declares That A Medal Be Made

At 5:30 on the evening of November 27, 1830, as St. Catherine was praying in the chapel, the Holy Virgin appeared to her for the second time, "Her head was covered with a white veil extended to her feet which rested on a half sphere, with her heel crushing the head of a serpent. The Holy Virgin holds a globe in her hands representing the whole world, and each person in particular, and offers it to God, imploring His mercy. She wears rings on her fingers, bearing precious stones that shed rays, one more beautiful than the next, symbolizing the graces that the Holy Virgin pours out on those who ask for them.

During the second apparition, Our Blessed Mother explained to St. Catherine "how pleased she is when people pray to her and how generous she is with them; how she gives special graces to those who ask; and what a great joy she takes in granting them." At that point "a frame formed around Our Lady, like an oval, bearing the following words in gold letters: 'O Mary, conceived without sin, pray for us who have recourse to thee.'" Then a voice was heard saying, "Have a medal struck after this model. Those who wear it, blessed, around their neck will receive great graces. The graces will be abundant for those who wear it with confidence."

After contemplating the picture on the medal, St. Catherine saw it turn to display the back. There she saw an "M," the monogram of Mary, surmounted by a small cross and, below it, the hearts of Jesus and Mary, the first surrounded with thorns and the latter pierced with a sword. Twelve stars surrounded the hearts and the monogram.

Confirming the predictions of St. Louis De Montfort, St. Catherine says that the Most Holy Virgin will be proclaimed Queen of the Universe: Oh! How beautiful it will be to hear: Mary is the Queen of the Universe. The children and everyone will cry with joy and rapture. That will be a lasting era of peace and happiness. She will be displayed on standards and paraded all over the world."

Prayer
O Mary, conceived without sin,
pray for us who have recourse to thee
and all those who do not have recourse to thee,
especially the enemies of the Church
and those in most need of mercy."

My Mother, My Confidence!

Brown Scapular & Sabbatine Privilege

The Brown Scapular is a sacramental of the Catholic Church and it is a part of the Habit of Carmel. It consists of two small pieces of brown material attached by string and is worn over the shoulders. The Brown Scapular originated on Mt. Carmel in the Holy Land near a cave of Elijah the Prophet, who has a great influence on the early members of Carmel.

The history of the Brown Scapular began with St. Simon Stock, who was the General of the Carmelite Order. Around the year 1251, when difficulties seemed insurmountable, St. Simon had recourse to the Blessed Virgin Mary, to whom he had great devotion. The Blessed Mother, in answer to his prayer appeared to him with the Brown Scapular in her hands saying, *"This shall be to you and all Carmelites a privilege, that anyone who dies clothed in this shall not suffer eternal fire; and if wearing it they die, they shall be saved."*

The Blessed Mother made the Scapular of the Carmelite Habit a sign of Her special love and pledge of Her motherly protection.

Catholic theologians and authorities like Vermeersch, St. Robert Bellarmine, Beringer, Pope Benedict XV, etc., explain the promise to mean that anyone dying in Mary's family (Carmelite

Order or Scapular Confraternity) will receive from Her, at the hour of death, either the grace of perseverance in the state of grace or the grace of final contrition.

Saints and Pontiffs have often warned us of the folly of abusing Mary's promise. At the same time that Pope Pius XI joyfully professed: "I learned to love the Scapular Virgin in the arms of my mother," he also warned the faithful that "…although it is very true that the Blessed Virgin loves all who love Her, nevertheless those who wish to have the Blessed Mother as a helper at the hour of death, must in life merit such a signal favor by abstaining from sin and laboring in Her honor."

It is unthinkable that anyone who deliberately sins, counting on Mary's Scapular Promise to save him will die clothed in the Scapular. To lead a willfully sinful life while trusting in the Scapular Promise is to commit a sin of presumption.

The "*Sabbatine (Saturday) Privilege* is based on a bull said to have been issued March 3, 1322 by Pope John XXII. This privilege is frequently understood to mean that those who wear the Scapular and fulfill two other conditions (which, according to the only copy of the bull in existence, were made by the Blessed Virgin in an apparition to Pope John XXII before he became Pope) will be freed from Purgatory on the first Saturday after death. Why Saturday, because in the Church's liturgical prayers for each day of the week, Saturday is the day that the Church celebrates in Her honor.

Conditions of Sabbatine Privilege

Conditions are:

1. Wear the Brown Scapular faithfully;
2. Observe chastity according to one's state in life;
3. Pray five decades of the Rosary daily, when substitution of the daily Rosary has been granted in place of the Little Office of the Blessed Virgin Mary. (It is also permitted by the Carmelite Order, which has authority over Scapular regulations to ask one's parish priest for permission to substitute the Rosary for the Little Office as a condition for obtaining the Sabbatine Privilege.)

To obtain the fullest possible benefits from the Brown Scapular devotion, one must be validly invested or enrolled in the Brown Scapular. A priest can invest a catholic by using the proper investiture in the Scapular. Once one is invested they are invested until death. In addition, once the first scapular has been blessed no other subsequent scapulars need to be blessed and it must be worn around the neck.

There has been a renewed devotion in wearing the Brown Scapular in our century due to Our Lady appearing in Fatima on October 13, 1917, as Our Lady of Mt. Carmel, holding out the Brown Scapular in Her hands. When Sr. Lucia was asked why Our Lady held the Scapular in Her hands, she answered, *"... because it is our sign of consecration to Her Immaculate Heart."*

In 1950, Pope Pius XII wrote the now famous words concerning the Scapular: *"Let it be your sign of consecration to the*

Immaculate Heart of Mary, which we are particularly urging in these perilous times."

On August 15, 1950, Sr. Lucia stated: *"The Rosary and the Scapular are inseparable."*

The Ritual of Investiture admits the one being invested to a participation "in all the Masses, prayers and good works performed by the religious of Mt. Carmel." This participation plus the great promise of salvation and the Sabbatine Privilege give an unspeakable spiritual value to the Brown Scapular devotion.

Suggestions for Further Reading

Secret of Mary, by St. Louis Marie De Montfort

The Secret of the Rosary, by St. Louis Marie De Montfort

The Glories of Mary, by St. Alphonsus Liguori

Aim Higher, by St. Maximilian Kolbe

All Generations Shall Call Me Blessed, by Fr. Stefano M. Manelli, F.F.I.

Rosary Meditations Loving Jesus with the Heart of Mary, Eucharistic Meditations on the Fifteen Mysteries of the Rosary, by Fr. Martin Lucia, SS.CC.

An Examination of Conscience a Preparation for the Sacrament of Penance, by Fr. Robert Altier